A **WESTERN HORSEMAN** I

BACKCOUNTRY BASICS

Your Guide to Solving Common Problems on the Trail

By Mike Kinsey with Jennifer Denison

Edited by
Fran Devereux Smith and Cathy Martindale

Photography by
John Brasseaux

Backcountry Basics

Published by
WESTERN HORSEMAN magazine
3850 North Nevada Ave.
Box 7980
Colorado Springs, CO 80933-7980
800-877-5278

www.westernhorseman.com

Design, Typography, and Production
Western Horseman
Fort Worth, Texas

Front and Back Cover Photos by
John Brasseaux

Printing
Branch Smith
Fort Worth, Texas

Manufactured in the United States of America

First Printing: September 2008

ISBN 978-0-911647-84-6

DEDICATION AND ACKNOWLEDGMENTS

As a youngster, I never thought of my father as being gifted. I assumed every horseman worked to bring out the best of each horse. Thirty-five years later "natural horsemanship" became a glossy pitch for what Dad called "working with" a horse.

Incredibly tough, but never harsh, my father was a quiet man whose words were loaded. He typically communicated with hand and body signals, perfectly suited to be a horseman. Others admired Dad's accomplishments with horses and said he had "the gift." His insight into equine psychology seemed natural to me.

He encouraged me to study such horsemen as Jesse Beery and Ralph Moody. My formal internship began at age 8; Dad never gave lessons, but demonstrated and critiqued. I can still hear Dad's trademark admonishment, his encouragement and his commandment: "Start 'em right." Shortchanging a horse by doing the easy thing violated Dad's commandment.

I dedicate this book to my father, my boyhood "Superman," who quietly but intently gave me a passion for horses. I regret that it took Dad's death for me to fully appreciate that he had given me "the gift."

Mom was a perfect fit for my father. Chatty, loving and warm, she always sacrificed for us kids, but never made it seem that way. We were her joy, and she instilled in us the pride to "do the right thing."

A sharp horsewoman, she never had Dad's passion for horses, but upstaged us often enough to keep us humble. To Mom, thanks not just for a book, but also for my life's direction.

Uncle Dan taught me to love life and the outdoors, and shared his family home during my college years. He taught me to regard mistakes as opportunities to learn and improve. I was devastated, when returning from Desert Storm, to find he'd passed away.

I'm blessed with a wife who has, for 28 years, not only endured my many faults, but also encouraged me when I was discouraged, offered me a hand when I have failed, and continued to love me when I was insufferable. To my wife, Jenny, thank you.

I thank my children, Jon and Jennifer, for their support. I never intended for them to retrain problem horses, but hard times build character. Both now demonstrate their character and conviction to duty, honor and their country. Jon recently graduated from the U.S. Air Force Academy and awaits pilot training. Jennifer just finished "Beast," or Academy basic training, as she starts her journey there. Thank you both for your dedication, as well as understanding. I love and respect you, and your mom and I miss you.

I thank my "other children," whom I've taught, mentored, fussed at and loved. Heather, like my own blood, shared rooms and pranks with Jennifer. Shanna, Mary Madison, Jessica, Brianna, Lauren, Kathy, Tanya, Patricia, Bianca, SeleAnna, Danae, Immy, Rebecca, Yasmine and other interns were bruised handling tough horses. Thanks for your help, patience and time, and for allowing me to share my father's passion.

Special thanks to Toni Laston, our ranch foreman, school director and good friend for many years. Toni has juggled responsibilities as a wife and mother of three to care for up to 100 head of horses, students and clinic and training schedules. I most appreciate her ability to soothe clients offended by my brusque "tell it like it is" style.

Another wonderfully talented lady has also become special to me. Jennifer Denison has remained sane and focused in spite of my writing style, or lack thereof. Patiently and skillfully, Jennifer has blended my thoughts and passion, when others would've thrown up their hands in defeat. Jennifer, you are an angel.

Ultimately, I thank the Lord for continued health and the talent and opportunity to experience crazy blessings—collapsing parachutes, snake bites, flying the North Atlantic in an old, single-engine plane with a pregnant wife, driving through war-torn Central America with my then-18-month-old son, misfiring explosives on the DMZ in Korea, riding horses through ice and swollen rivers, being on a "Hail Mary" during Desert Storm. All are evidence the Lord cares for those who do the foolish. Thank you, Lord, for giving this old fool so many second chances and so many friends with whom to share.

CONTENTS

FOREWORD

Toni Laston

Almost 10 years ago I had a 10-year-old Quarter Horse gelding, Black, who carried baggage from being handled by novices. I'd grown up with horses, confident in my riding abilities, but had never dealt with these particular behavioral issues. Frustrated, I looked for professional help and found Mike.

Mike came to my farm to watch Black and me interact before commenting. Any given day, Black might lead willingly—or not. He led beautifully for five steps, then became a brick wall. I grimaced and said, "Here's where I get frustrated and feel like a total failure."

Mike smiled, asking me to unhalter Black. I wasn't as attuned to equine body language then as I am now, so missed the conversation as Mike approached my horse. However, Mike didn't allow Black's customary nudging as he again was haltered. When Mike cued Black, the horse magically responded, walking around the paddock. They stopped, backed and walked again. For a moment, I was sure Mike had performed a magic mojo on Black.

I became aware of Mike's subtle corrections—a raised elbow telling the horse to maintain his distance or a gentle bump to go forward. Ultimately, I realized a dialog was occurring and determined that I needed lessons in horse language. The amazing part:

Most people could've missed everything that occurred between Mike and Black. Had I not been desperate to understand my failure, I, too, might've missed the exchange.

Later, I began Train the Trainer lessons with Mr. Mike, as he's known, and quickly developed my horsemanship skills. Then I began working as foreman of his Start 'Em Right program—a rewarding experience.

Mike's philosophy is about building a realistic working relationship with horses. His knowledge of starting young horses is unsurpassed. Clinicians offer useful tips, but none have shown me how to recognize my horse's issue on "this day" or how to recognize a potential issue like Mike has. One of Mike favorite's lines: "Every time you're with your horse, you teach him something good or something bad." And he practices what he preaches.

His horses begin training as foals, and they are then turned out for a few months. Later, training starts right where it stopped. Because their initial human interaction has been quality training time, these young horses aren't frustrated by not understanding their roles in horse-human relationships.

As Mike's program has evolved, we've seen a need for business-minded trail horses and, most importantly, that people need an understanding of horse psychology. To increase the probability of enjoying horses safely, you must have the necessary skills. Mike has dedicated much of his career to helping people attain such skills, so he was thrilled to do the "Backcountry Basics" series for *Western Horseman* in 2003. The straightforward series addressed trail-riding issues and provided simple, easy-to-follow steps that helped people solve problems. Inspired by the series, this book shares information from the articles and a glimpse into the making of a trail horse.

I've enjoyed every moment of this book's culmination since readers finally have the opportunity to spend time with a real horseman. I'm so honored to have been the opening voice in a book that will change people's perspective on horsemanship. Enjoy the ride!

Toni Laston
Foreman
Start 'Em Right!

INTRODUCTION

Mike Kinsey runs his Train the Trainer and Start 'Em Right horse-training programs from his farm in Belton, S.C.

Respectfully Speaking

Countless times I've seen horse owners try new techniques they've learned at clinics. I watch their frustration grow as their horses don't respond to the methods the way they did during the clinics. It's more painful for me to watch the horses become intimidated, frustrated, angry or even afraid in response to what they perceive to be pointless, almost abusive activity.

I don't want this book to contribute to that trend, so I encourage you not to skip this introduction. It might contain the most important keys to your comprehension, and therefore, your horse's understanding, responsiveness and success. Applying techniques without first understanding a horse's motivation is like throwing dice—it comes down to luck. I firmly believe horses deserve our best, and guessing and gambling is not what I consider good horsemanship.

Respect

Through the years, I've wondered what happened to respectful manners in horses and people. In the late 1950s, I remember seeing horses tied to trailers and hitching posts, or placed in catch pens, after riding. The horses stood quietly, snoozing and flipping their tails at flies. You didn't see them pawing the ground, chewing on lead ropes, kicking at people or other animals, rearing or otherwise misbehaving. When they were handled and ridden, they weren't threats, and they certainly didn't bite, kick or jostle their riders. Most horses back then respected their handlers and the handlers' space, thereby providing less opportunity for people to get hurt.

I remember the first time I was allowed to ride my family's King Ranch-bred stallion and rope calves for the older guys to brand, castrate and vaccinate. Even though I was only 8 years old and was so small I had to climb the fender to get into the saddle, the old cutting-bred stallion respectfully listened to my requests. He not only did what I asked, but also listened for my cues. He also didn't "talk" to the mares tied around the pen. When I dropped my reins on the horse's neck to prepare my lariat, he continued to quietly follow and push a calf to the outside of the herd, where I could swing my loop and make a clean catch.

I knew better than to charge the horse around the pen, chasing calves. Instead, we slunk quietly through the herd. I learned early that the right thing—the respectful thing—was to be careful and not needlessly hurt God's creatures or run off any fat. Thin calves generated little money, which meant slim pickin's at the dinner table. Just as the stallion always respected my wishes, I was learning respect, and I respected my parents' teaching, and I respected the ranch environment.

Try to remember the last time you attended an event where children or horses sat or stood quietly, respectfully waiting for their parents or handlers, respectively. I remember reaching for a second piece of pie at a potluck, and feeling one of my dad's thick, calloused fingers tapping me on the head. When I looked into his face, he just shook his head. Without any questions, I left the pie alone. Later, in private, Dad explained that not everyone had eaten yet, teaching me a lesson in being considerate of others, whatever the situation.

Before I was 5 years old, my mom taught me that gentlemen walked on the street side of the sidewalk to protect the ladies, opened doors without being asked and offered to carry ladies' packages. We might not have had running water in our old farmhouse until I was 16, but we had respect for others, and we took pride in our respectful manners and in the respectful manners of our horses.

That attention to detail, that respectful watching and listening, developed because my parents were proud of their children and their horses. They didn't want us embarrassing ourselves or needlessly hurting ourselves.

Respectful manners in horses have become so rare that I have to demonstrate them at clinics. People think it's a trick when I walk through a gate, leading a horse with a loose lead or rein, and the horse stops at a gate while I unlatch or unchain it, then moves out of the gate's way, again with no guidance from me, and finally, turns to follow the gate as I close it. That's no trick—my horse just knows the respect I learned as a youngster.

Respect might be more important in trail riding than any other discipline due to the unpredictability of obstacles, terrain, weather and other trail users. Some riders might mistake their horses' reluctance or rebellion at obstacles, fidgeting on the trail, spooking, charging, kicking and a host of other issues for "problems." Many times, these issues aren't problems at all, but merely symptoms of a lack of respect for human leadership. Horses that have been raised or trained in a compromising or permissive environment can have many or all these symptoms of lack of respect for human leadership. A trail horse that lacks respect for his handler tends to busy himself making decisions instead of listening for rider guidance. A good trail horse knows he's a member of the team and has learned to trust the rider's judgment and concerns himself instead with placing his feet and executing the rider's directions. Horses treated as pets have a preoccupation with their own learned self-importance and believe they're equal or even senior partners. They continually question their riders' judgment, and constantly jeopardize their own and their riders' safety.

Manners and Safety

Riding a horse with good manners is like driving a car with an automatic transmission,

as opposed to a manual shift. Once directed, the horse should follow through without constant shifting and adjusting. Good manners indicate respect for authority, or "listening," which leads to increased control and safety.

A few years ago, I was hauling seven horses in our reverse-load stock trailer to a mountain trail site. I was buzzing along a rural highway when an older fellow in a pickup pulled out in front of me. With a car coming from the other direction and steep shoulders along the road, I had no choice but to suddenly hit the brakes. The subsequent slamming noise in the trailer didn't surprise me. We missed the pickup, and after I smoked the vehicle to a stop, my assistant, Toni Laston, and I jumped out of the truck and looked into the trailer. Two horses that had been loaded toward the center of the trailer were down. Their ties had broken, and they had slid forward, under the other horses. The forward-loaded horses were straddling the fallen horses. There was no blood, no obvious injuries, and, most importantly, no thrashing, angry or panicked horses.

We jumped back into the truck and drove a few hundred feet so we could park the trailer off the road. We unloaded all the standing horses, and then I inspected the fallen horses. It was apparent we'd escaped any real damage. I bumped one of the horses with my toe to get him up, while Toni began putting a new lead on the halter. A similar command elicited a similar response from the second horse. Other than broken leads, there was no damage, no broken legs, no horses to be put down and nothing to doctor.

Amazingly the two horses just lay there under the standing horses. None of them flailed around, insisted on their comfort or demanded they do what they wanted to do. It was obvious from their eyes and their faces they weren't wild about my new training technique, but they respectfully repressed their instinctual reaction and waited for me to help them. The standing horses hadn't kicked, reared or rebelled at straddling the horses under them. Toni and I reloaded them all and went on to have another day our clients would remember not as a day horses were injured, crippled or put down, but rather as an enjoyable trail ride. The outcome wasn't predicated by luck, but rather by proper preparation due to appropriate horsemanship.

I recall a woman questioning my mounting an inexperienced trail prospect while tied to a trailer. She thought such a technique was dangerous. If it's too dangerous for me to mount a horse tied to my trailer, the horse is too dangerous to be ridden. Tying or being otherwise restrained, and willingly submitting to the handler or rider's will is basic. If your horse is too dangerous to tie and mount, you need to get some basic horsemanship help before you get hurt.

Attitude

I believe one of the important facets of horsemanship is a willing attitude. I've never seen a rider or owner criticize a pleasant-acting horse. But few people seem to realize they're accountable for their horses' attitudes. I see riding and training programs, university teaching programs and even various sport associations fail to address the importance of equine attitude.

Teaching programs commonly instruct riders on the various "what to do" mechanics of training, such as how to get a horse on the correct lead, what to do to side-pass or how to collect a horse. Those same programs might never consider teaching a horse that it's wrong to threaten the rider or handler.

An important, even crucial, difference with my Start 'Em Right program is that we teach a rider or handler three facets leading to a willing attitude. First, we teach the person to be observant of what the horse is doing. Second, we teach him to recognize not just what the horse is doing, but why the horse is doing it. And third, we teach that addressing attitude, or "how" the horse is doing, always takes priority over training the "what."

Horsemanship

Months ago, I read a book review that claimed horsemanship was at an all-time high. My observations of horses and riders at clinics, events and trail rides demonstrate just the opposite. In the 50 years I've been riding and training, I see horsemanship of the recreational rider, and even many professional riders, becoming increasingly misconstrued. At the top tier of the performance-horse industry, horsemanship has improved, at least in the arena. However, some performance horses' behavior going into a trailer, maintaining a respectful space, leading and tying, and their general ground manners often leaves much to be desired.

As a culture, we want things to happen easily and instantly. Learning training techniques is easy, but learning horsemanship requires attention to detail, focus, commitment, and, in essence, hard work. Therefore, in spite of the lip service, horsemanship is neglected.

I define horsemanship simply as the relationship of respect, communication and cooperation between the horse and his rider or handler. To attempt to judge the horsemanship of the rider or handler without considering the horse and the relationship is merely naïve and empty. In Western riding, knowledgeable folks recognize that the equine ballet called reining is the pinnacle of horsemanship. In the opening paragraphs for any reining rulebook you find the words "the horse should be willingly guided or controlled with little or no apparent resistance and dictated to completely." A horse that pins his ears, conveying a threat to his rider, refuses to go forward, runs sideways, bounces his rear, wrings his tail in irritation or displays an overall poor attitude is not being guided willingly.

There's no reason trail riders should tolerate poor attitudes in their horses. One would think, due to the market blitz selling horsemanship programs, systems, clinics, videos, television programs and assorted gimmicks, that recognizing solid horsemanship and effective training would be easy. I think assuming such is a mistake. Some observations that indicate the meaning of horsemanship has been misconstrued:

- the increasing number of horse-related emergency-room trauma;

- self-professed backyard trainers offering poor quality, and sometimes detrimental, "help" via public horse forums, as well as those lulled into reading and using those training "tips;"

- forum participants speaking in terms of marketing catch phrases, rather than horses' actions, reactions and behaviors;

- clinicians selling programs of low-stress, low-resistance or other polarized, sound-good marketing titles, phrases and check lists, rather than programs based on recognizing and understanding horses' behavior and psychology;

- instructors teaching riding without having the knowledge to deal with the horse problems related to their teaching;

- nationally known event organizations with horsemanship judges officiating solely on how the riders sit and ride, unaware of and unconcerned with the interaction between each horse and rider.

Motivation

Too often we're in such a rush to become more successful, productive and safer with our horses that we jump for what appears to be the easiest solution. Attempting to apply techniques without learning basic horsemanship principles often means we apply techniques at the wrong time, in the wrong situation or don't apply them correctly. Consequently, our horses become unruly, frustrated and dangerous.

Techniques that might apply to a fearful horse could merely encourage worse behavior in a horse with disrespectful, familiarity issues. Likewise, appropriate techniques for the disrespectful-familiar horse would further traumatize the fearful horse. We must recognize the horse's motivation. To recognize the motivation, we must care enough to give a horse our attention. We must listen with our eyes, and then must care enough to learn the horse's language. We must become so familiar with equine body language that we know what a horse is telling us. Only then can we begin to apply the right training techniques at the right times.

We also must develop the courage to do what is right for a horse's long-term well-being, and not make decisions based on our emotional reactions. Just as some mothers might not let their sons play football, compete on the track team or wrestle in high school, some horse owners are unreasonably protective. Keeping blankets on horses in 70-degree weather because an afternoon rain might come up is not doing what's best for the horse. Horses, like children, must play, make mistakes and reap consequences for poor decisions in order to grow, develop and mature into useful, productive members of our society.

Selecting a Trainer

Conventional wisdom given on many public horse forums is to "pick a trainer who shares your training philosophy." I find such advice ludicrous.

If your training philosophy is poorly grounded, you might get exactly the "expertise" you desire. The result often might be a poorly trained horse, or a horse with a poor attitude and poor manners. Your horse deserves better than that.

Get smart about training, and specifically about starting young horses. Otherwise, you handicap your horse for the remainder of his life. Your likes and dislikes don't necessarily have anything to do with good training. Learn to recognize the results of sound training and capable trainers. Not everyone can be a painter, a sculptor, an artist or a horse trainer. Recognize your limitations, and remember that seeking good help, learning proper techniques, and working slowly and patiently are always cheaper than risking injury to yourself, your horse or others. The sooner you realize that, the sooner you're on your way to enjoying worry-free trail rides.

1

THE START 'EM RIGHT EVOLUTION

I wasn't one of those guys who grew up dreaming of being a cowboy. I knew up close and personal what it was like to grab a calf for vaccinating or branding and end up on the bottom, in several inches of manure, while the rascal kicked skin off my body. I became a horseman at an early age, and learned that the more one knows, the more one can learn.

I was 8 when my dad decided my riding for fun needed to become more productive. He suggested readings from books by professor Jesse Beery and Ralph Moody, as well as articles from the *Quarter Horse Journal*, *Western Horseman* and other magazines. After I studied the writings, he quizzed me, had me demonstrate starting colts, and asked why one acted in a certain

This photo of my dad, taken in the mid-1940s, is one of the few I have of him horseback. When it was too wet to hay cattle with a truck, Dad carried bales, one at a time, on this horse, Pard.

This yearling filly was an example of the Quarter Horse foals we raised.

manner while another did something else. These questions began my lifelong quest into the "why" of horse psychology. Dad called this "working with the horse," in lieu of forcing or fighting the horse. This was my foundation of horse psychology, which, decades later, I'd hear popularly marketed as "natural horsemanship."

My internship with my dad continued for several years. By the time I was 10, I started all my family's colts, and the following year I began starting colts for area ranches. I could always expect questions from Dad regarding why different horses acted in different ways, and how I adjusted to bring each horse along successfully. This early immersion into horse psychology and the question, "Why?" has been a blessing in all aspects of my life, although it's often an irritant to others.

I continue to be motivated to learn every day. The questioning attitude my dad began developing when I was young likely will cease when my heart quits beating. As a gray-headed man, I also recognize that a large number of folks can't—or won't—learn because they already know all they want to know. But if you're open to new ideas, you continue to grow as a horseman and enjoy many pleasant miles on your horse.

Training Principles

Below are some of the most valuable lessons I learned about horses and training from my dad and the horses I've worked. The principles still apply to my training program.

Principle 1: Every time you handle a horse, be aware of what he's learning. Violating this rule is usually the cause of a horse losing respect for his handler. Every time you get close to a horse, you train him. He doesn't take a day off from learning. If you don't have a plan for training, you can bet your horse will learn things you hadn't planned.

Principle 2: No matter what your training objective is for a particular horse on any given day, correcting behavioral issues always becomes the priority. For example, your training objective might be to work at getting a horse to collect, move his ribs or his hind end off your leg cues, or something else. If the horse decides to cow kick or bounce around, taking control, or just pins his ears and appears threatening, deal with his attitude before you start your day's training agenda.

Once his attitude or misbehavior has been handled, the horse will show his willingness to learn. Then you can continue with your training objective.

Before you do any training maneuver with a horse, however, get his attention, respect and willing cooperation. It's not enough that he does what you ask; he also must be attentive, act respectfully and be willing. To ignore poor behavior is to allow it to become acceptable, and you should never settle for that.

Principle 3: Fighting a horse is counterproductive, but allowing him to fuss or fight with himself gives the horse the opportunity to think through his situation. Turning a horse out in a paddock with a saddle, bridle or a tarp on the ground gives him a chance to work through his concerns. Restraining a horse by tying or hobbling allows him to decide to be comfortable and submissive or to be uncomfortable and sweaty. This promotes the horse learning to do the right thing.

Years ago, I found a parallel when my 3-year-old daughter didn't want to wear clothes. My giving in because the tantrums were unpleasant did not solve anything. Often the best way for an individual to figure out the right thing is to let him throw tantrums, without removing him from the situation, until he decides that tantrums don't work. If, as many horse owners do, I had given in to the tantrums, my now 18-year-old daughter wouldn't be at the Air Force Academy.

Principle 4: Every horse is an individual to be treated with respect and understanding. Each one has strengths, weaknesses, fears, suspicions and, occasionally, reckless boldness. These characteristics vary not only from horse to horse, but also within the same horse on a given day, depending on energy level, weather, diet, surroundings, confidence, concern, fear, nervousness or other mental state. Don't get so fixed on your training plan that you can't adjust to issues that arise.

Principle 5: An effective trainer sets up a horse for success. For example, avoid trying to teach a horse to stand still when he's full of nervous energy. It's better to teach him when his mind is conducive to focusing and learning. The end of a training session is a much more appropriate time to teach him to stand still. This was part of Dad's training

Punch Stone, our herd stallion, was respectful enough that I could handle him when I was 5 years old.

and horsemanship principle: "Don't fight the horse." The training needs to occur, but pick a time when the horse is ready to learn. Think of teaching children. Do you really want to say, "No don't do that, don't, no, stop, no, no, no?" Better to direct the child by saying, "Go

I waited until Dad left for work to find out how broke a new horse might be. Dad's note on back of the photo says that Mr. Robin consistently dumped my cousins. I had to climb on the fence to bridle him, but with a little "defensive riding," the stallion was a gem for cow work.

People warned that Cotulla Brown Ribbon, a grandson of Peppy #212, the 1934 Quarter Horse stallion, was a killer. Soon, we kids rode the stallion with no halter or bridle. Even my mom got on the horse.

do this, okay, move there, step over here, get away from my space, now do this." Set up the training to avoid punishing the horse for things you shouldn't reasonably expect him to perform.

Principle 6: Allowing a horse to repeat poor behavior builds bad habits, which can become lifelong baggage. Conversely, permitting a horse to make a mistake, and then correcting him, is a positive training procedure. But a trainer who repeatedly makes the same mistakes is sloppy, uncaring, and inexcusable. Dad's philosophy was: "If at first you don't succeed, figure out what's going wrong and fix it!"

Principle 7: We never punish instinctual actions, such as spooking or otherwise being frightened, distracted or playful. But we never tolerate and we do discipline for behavioral actions, such as rebellious cow-kicking, bucking, pulling against the lead or reins, or otherwise attempting to punish or bully the human handler.

Principle 8: Teaching a horse to go, stop, turn, back and do other maneuvers is wasted effort if the horse doesn't do it willingly. Think of teaching him to want to do something, which is a long-term benefit. Forcing a horse to do something is a short-term solution that eventually fails the horse and rider. Dad made it very clear that failing a horse indicates a trainer's failure. He had no use for ignorance, arrogance or a lack of caring. The ranch amply demonstrated what happened to failures. If one needed to use tough love and ensure an animal's long-term well-being, anything less than what was needed was considered a failure.

Dad usually ended these principles with encouragement to take them to my heart and soul. His encouragement, his commandment and his his admonishment: "Start 'em right!" This principle is so deeply ingrained that it pains me to watch others routinely handle their horses in a manner motivated to bring gratification to themselves, rather than success to their horses.

Ultimately, I spend less overall time teaching horses raised here in the Start 'Em Right environment, because they understand that their jobs are to learn, and they don't just wait to be taught. I watch for a similar attitude from students and interns. Do I have to stop and spend my time teaching every aspect of horsemanship, or does the individual have the self-discipline to watch and learn? If, for every small process, I must stop and spend time teaching that two-legged or four-legged student, I can't accomplish much. I have total lifetime concern for my horses' welfare, so I consequently spend much more time in the beginning, teaching the individual that it's his or her responsibility to learn, to focus on being attentive, to willingly cooperate and to be respectful. Spending that extra time initially, while holding the individual responsible for himself or herself, pays big dividends when the student participates successfully in the learning process.

Our Start 'Em Right program produces cooperative, respectful horse-and-rider teams.

Leading the Way

Horsemanship and leadership have many correlations. Developing individuals to be successful can be much more involved and much more rewarding, and have more long-term benefits than just teaching "do what I say."

I appreciate that a judged performance horse needs to know the cues for lead changes, but I expect my trail horses to know what to do without directives from me. If I'm loping to the left, I want him on the left lead, and if I'm loping right, I want him on the right lead. When I go straight, I don't care about the lead. I want to focus on the cow I'm following, limbs that I'm ducking, or the ditch or ravine I'm jumping. I want my horse in the automatic-transmission mode. Most of all, I want his attention, cooperation and respect.

After all these years, I still love horses—all horses. I never tire of watching them play. Nothing is as satisfying to me as having a young horse respond to instruction with a willing attitude, or a mature horse listening intently as we buzz through a narrow brushy trail at a fast trot, dodging limbs and vines with leg cues.

I am, however, deeply disturbed by the compromising familiarity between horses and humans that's promoted by so many. It's so pervasive I find actual abuse by humans insignificant by comparison. It's easy to blame marketing, but what the public wants is what sells. As long as horse owners want to believe the myth of "love them, and they'll love back," that familiarity is more important than respect, and want to "feel good" rather than be responsible, that's what marketing gurus will sell, and horses will continue to suffer. I see an epidemic that frightens and saddens me. My hope is that this book spares a few horses' suffering. Horse psychology might be a science, but applying it is an art, and that's what you learn in the next chapter, "Inside Your Horse's Mind."

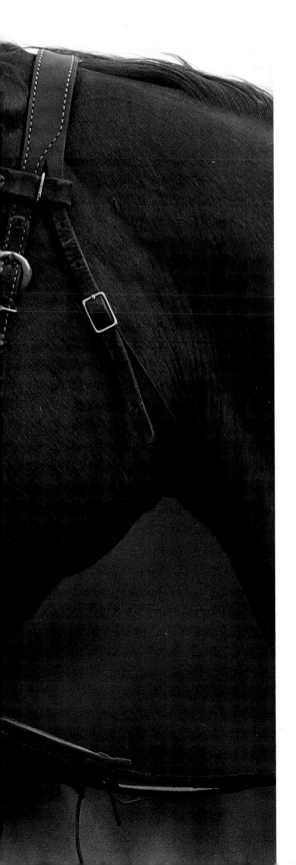

Learn what your horse's body language is telling you, so you can apply the correct training technique.

2

INSIDE YOUR HORSE'S MIND

Horse psychology, in my vernacular, is recognizing what a horse is doing and why he's doing it. Plus, you must apply horsemanship principles and appropriate techniques to encourage him to act as a productive reliable team member, or to cease doing anything that interferes with that. Applying techniques without understanding a horse's motivation, also known as the "why," is gambling, which is not good or consistent with horsemanship.

Horse owners react differently to horse-psychology discussions. A woman once told me, "Horse training isn't brain surgery." Her comment does have merit, but not as she intended. I've noticed there are many more inexperienced horse owners training horses than there are uninformed doctors doing brain surgery. Not knowing how to do something, or not knowing a quality result from just a result, makes it difficult to recognize the difference. The longer an individual—two- or four-legged—has been doing something, the more difficult it is to get that person or animal to change without a traumatic event.

It takes more than years of horse ownership to be a horseman. As with any art, natural talent, dedication and a willingness to learn and improve play big roles. You must be able to observe, focus and pay attention to details. Besides watching a horse, you must also "hear" with your eyes what his body language tells you. I've noticed at clinics that some people have trouble observing and recognizing what their horses are saying. The riders either don't observe, or fail to recognize, that their horses are displaying rude, threatening and potentially dangerous gestures and behaviors.

Once you focus on your horse, you must learn to interpret what he's "saying" with his body language. You can't accurately consider the training principle involved, and several different techniques that might apply, without understanding why they might be appropriate in a given situation.

Motivation Matters

Too often we're in such a rush to become successful, productive and safe with our horses that we jump for what appears to be an easy solution. Attempting to apply techniques without learning the underlying horsemanship principles often leads to using techniques at the wrong time or applying them incorrectly. Consequently, horses can become unruly, frustrated and dangerous.

Techniques that you might apply to a fearful horse could merely encourage worse behavior in a horse with disrespectful-familiarity issues. Likewise, appropriate techniques for a disrespectful-familiar horse could further traumatize a fearful horse. You need to recognize a horse's motivation before selecting a training technique. To recognize the motivation, you must care enought to give a horse your attention and listen with your eyes. You also need to care enough to become fluent in the horse's language. Observing the language and interpreting the motivation correctly are key to applying the appropriate training technique at the right time.

You also must develop the courage to do what's best for the horse's long-term well-being, and not make decisions based on emotional reaction. Just as some mothers might not let their sons play sports, some horse owners are unreasonably protective. Horses, like children, must play, make mistakes and reap consequences for poor decisions to become productive members of our society. Horses that fail to learn the consequences of misbehavior when they're youngsters are doomed to learn them as adults.

Motivation also matters when getting advice. Question whether the person at an equine forum is trying to assist you or to build his or her ego. Is the salesman really trying to help you and/or help your horse or sell you another signature gimmick?

Attitude Adjustments

I believe one of the most important facets of horsemanship is recognizing a willing attitude. No one criticizes a pleasant, willing horse, but few riders realize they're accountable for their horses' attitudes. I see riding programs, training programs, university teaching programs and even sport associations failing to address the importance of equine attitude.

Teaching programs commonly instruct riders on the various how-to mechanics of training, such as what to do to get a horse to depart on the correct lead, side-pass and collect. Those programs never consider teaching a horse that it's wrong to threaten the handler, probably because the professor or instructor doesn't recognize the threats.

A critical difference at my farm is that we teach students three facets that contribute to a willing attitude. First, we teach the person to observe what the horse is doing. Second, we show the person how to recognize not only what the horse is doing, but also why he's doing it. And third, we teach that addressing the attitude, or the "how" a horse is doing, always takes priority over training the "what."

Don't discount the damage done by some backyard breeder, which influences a young horse from birth. If the horse is raised with a self-centered attitude, the best trainer in the world can play only the hand he's dealt.

Manners, Safety and Trust

As I mentioned in the introduction of this book, riding a respectfully mannered horse is similar to driving a vehicle with automatic transmission. You don't need to constantly cue, or "shift," to maneuver the horse for various "driving conditions." Your horse should be attuned to your body language and his surroundings so that he can adjust his position accordingly. If your horse understands he's responsible for listening and complying, you are a safer team.

Consider loading a horse in a trailer without excessive cueing, keeping your horse on the correct lead without steady leg pressure or asking your horse to stand tied without pawing or rubbing. On the ranch or in a working environment, a horseman doesn't have time to ponder whether his horse is a help or a hindrance. Good behavior is required, not just desired. Assuming this mentality can be a crucial part of your horse's development. Willingly complying, listening and submitting are all traits of a respectful, well-mannered, safe horse. Using games and gimmicks as a substitute for good horsemanship might be easier or make you feel better, but can be of disservice to your horse and his longevity as a trail mount.

Trust from horses is not natural; it's both earned and nurtured, or it isn't present at all. Once you develop your horse's confidence, you can quickly lose it if you violate his trust and injure or frighten him. Respect begins naturally, but it can be easily lost and replaced with familiarity, which is a negative trait of a horse-and-rider team, because that can lead to disrespect and carelessness.

Foals are born naturally intimidated and even afraid of humans. Fear is a form of respect that's merely a matter of prey (the horse) and predator (the human). A good trainer nurtures that respect and prevents it from manifesting into fear, developing a confident, cooperative, watchful form of respect.

Horse owners typically go astray raising and training young horses, either by replacing respect with familiarity, resulting in what we might call pasture "pets," or occasionally with training programs that go 180 degrees the other way and replace respect with hatred.

Hateful Horses

I've encountered few hateful horses during the past 50 years, so I'll only briefly discuss that. Though hateful horses are by far the smallest category of problem horses with which I have dealt, they're the most violent and the most inherently dangerous. The course of action I recommend is to remove

Besides watching a horse, you must also be able to interpret what his body language tells you so you can apply the correct training technique.

A horse's language is best learned by watching him interact in a herd setting.

genetically hateful or extremely willful horses and their parents from the gene pool.

The environmentally produced, or taught and trained, hateful horses typically result from poor training programs, rather than novice owners. In my experience, horses that fall in this category are generally speed-event horses, such as barrel-racing, team-roping and mounted-shooting horses. Some competitors in these disciplines are motivated only by speed and demand it from their horses by using spurs, whips and other devices. At the same time, tie-downs, harsh bits and other gimmicks restrain and restrict their horses.

I conclude that riders who are focused on winning now, rather than considering their horses' long-term development, push their young horses to perform beyond the horses' capabilities. Young horses are more easily manipulated than mature horses, so it stands to reason that youngsters initially can

be bullied and abused into submission by pain, intimidation and fear. As these horses mature, their intimidation is replaced by hatred. When I get a 5- to 6-year-old roping horse that stands in the round pen, eyes me with no visible emotion, no fear, no respect, and no cooperation, I know to be very careful. A horse like this has learned to tolerate abuse to a point. When you cross that horse's perceived point of abuse, the response can be so quick, violent and intent on doing harm that it's difficult to escape.

Self-Centered Horses

A "pet" horse has lost his natural respect for any leadership, has a preoccupation with his own learned self-importance and believes he's an equal or even senior "partner" on your team. He constantly questions your judgment and jeopardizes your and his safety. Likewise, a horse led by a foolishly naïve handler isn't

If a horse becomes too familiar with your presence and starts pushing into your space, as this Paint has, it can lead to a loss of respect and the horse taking advantage of you.

inclined to foolishly follow. With time, you can learn to recognize a spoiled horse by the way he's constantly disciplined, threatened, bitten, kicked and bullied by other horses in the herd. Being banged around for lacking respect is not the same as ranking low in the pecking order. People, due to the abdication of their duty to animals, have exposed many horses to a lifetime of suffering. Too often, people want to be buddies or partners with their horses, or establish a loving bond, and consequently expose their horses to needless suffering.

Many people can visualize their neighbor babying a horse to the point the horse becomes a pet accustomed to being pampered. That's another avenue to producing a horse with his own priority. The following is an e-mail I received regarding a horse's progress. I deleted names to avoid offending the involved parties.

"My horse did great when we saddled her (for the fifth time, no longer flipping over). She stood and walked out quietly. I decided to put bug spray on her, having already sprayed her twice before, and she exploded, bucking, rearing and falling over. When she quieted down, I eventually unsaddled her and she walked away quietly. I'm still concerned about getting out in the open with her, because she just explodes when she doesn't like something."

This horse wasn't "pampered" by petting and treats. She developed a self-centered attitude as she grew up, due to a handler who avoided discipline and failed to allow consequences for confrontational behavior. This horse is well-bred with a world-caliber cutting pedigree. So why the violent objection at each addition to the training program?

I have seen it a hundred times before. This filly never suffered consequences for throwing tantrums as a foal, so continues to have tantrums whenever she disagrees with training. The filly is much more likely to injure herself now than if she had been tied as a foal. Just as children who are not corrected for throwing tantrums continue as adults, so do horses. When we refuse to tie a young horse, and we use gimmicks such as bungees, tubes and "ringthings," we set up a horse for injuries later in life. But if we allow a horse to pay his dues as a youngster, we can minimize his trauma in the long run.

Horses that arrive for training at our facility go through an intensive, sometimes extended, boot camp. It can take weeks or even months to convince a horse that his job is not to decide what training he likes or rejects. Once these nasty, self-centered thoughts are in a horse's mind, they're never erased and, at best, are managed.

Trainer Selection

When dealing with problem horses, it's a good idea to get help before you get hurt. Before you invest time and money selecting a trainer, take time to reflect on your own horsemanship skills. Identify what you don't know, or don't have in your own repertoire of skills. Understand that you might have to move out of your comfort zone for your horse's long-term well-being.

Avoid trainers who offer quick fixes. Realize that if you want training and solutions that last your horse's lifetime, you must continue the training you pay for, or you nullify the training as your horse learns to manipulate you. Consider that your training philosophy might not have sufficient validity, particularly if it's passed on in movies or feel-good marketing campaigns. Trainers who understand natural horsemanship should be able to explain what's natural versus the unnatural and the ill-advised practices making the rounds today.

Conventional wisdom given on many public horse forums is to "pick a trainer who shares your training philosophy." I find this advice ludicrous. If your training philosophy is poorly grounded, you gain nothing because you might well get exactly the same poorly grounded "expertise" you desire. The result often can be a poorly trained horse, or a horse with a poor attitude and poor manners. Your horse deserves better than that.

If you go to a clinic or to see a trainer, don't be seduced by showmanship and entertainment. Handling a polished horse is not as helpful as seeing a horseman handle a problem horse. Tutor yourself to watch the horse's actions and reactions. When the clinician or trainer markets his or her program, watch to see if the demo horse is quietly watching and waiting to cooperate, or if the clinician allows the horse to bump into him, invade his space or otherwise exhibit poor manners.

Not everyone has the talent, experience or insight to be an artist, musician or trainer. Recognize your limitations and the limitations of those offering you advice.

Common Trail-Riding Errors

The common errors I see on the trail, from both Western and English riders are:

1. Arguing with a horse. If your horse is running backward, sideways or bouncing up and down, you can't make him stand still. Loosen your reins or lead rope so he can move his feet, and guide him in the direction you can make him go. If you're pulling on the reins, the lead rope or saddle horn, you need help. Get over the ego, and work to become a better horseman.

2. Using force. Trying to force a horse can result in someone or a horse getting hurt. The right bit, spur or whip used in a proper manner can be beneficial, but too often riders reach for one of these aids when they need to seek professional help. Bits, spurs and whips don't train horses, and although bits themselves aren't abusive, bits in the wrong hands can be. My typical response when a horse wants to fight during a training session is to get off, and with a snaffle, bit the horse 20 degrees to one side, letting him resist the pressure he's creating if he's so inclined. A human fighting with a horse is foolish, but a horse fighting with himself soon figures out who's the fool.

3. Giving cues a horse doesn't understand. I see folks on the trail clutching two reins in one hand, trying to neck rein an out-of-control horse. Maybe they're afraid they'll look like a rookie if they put a rein in each hand. Whatever their reasoning, giving cues to a horse, which he doesn't understand, or with which he's unwilling to comply, is not just a wasted effort, but also teaches the horse to further ignore your direction. Pulling with two reins might seem logical to a frightened novice, and a person can ride for 30 years and still demonstrate novice skills, but pulling on two reins doesn't gain control. Forget about trying to look like John Wayne, and learn how to get a rein in each hand and reclaim control, one rein at a time.

4. Compromising with a horse. This is a fool's game, and it always comes back to haunt you. If you reward a horse for doing something poorly, you continue to get poor responses, and eventually someone gets hurt.

One of the most important aspects of horsemanship is recognizing a willing attitude.

If your horse is pushing you around, seek help. Not doing so creates a spoiled horse, which defeats the purpose of horse ownership—to enjoy him. My refusal to teach one-rein-stops is not due to my disagreement with the concept, but rather the execution. Novices who use the one-rein-stop usually end up rewarding the horse for bad or uncontrollable behavior. Think about it: The horse gets the stop, and while the person talks to himself and his horse, letting the human heart slow down, getting his own shaking under control—the horse rests. I consider resting the horse the ultimate reward. So the horse behaves poorly and the rider gives him a rest break. As some of our young interns are so fond of saying, "Duh!"

5. Trying to make a horse stand still. You and I can't make a horse stand still while he's alive. So why set yourself up for failure? Turn your horse loose. If he's moving, don't "let" him move; instead, direct him to move, and keep him moving where you direct him to go. When you finally ask him to stop, he agrees with an "about time" attitude. Then reward him by standing for 20 to 30 seconds. If he

tenses, gets distracted and acts as though he's thinking of going, don't let him go; instead, make him go, directing him to turn, change direction and go wherever you want until he's ready for you to ask him to stop and rest. Don't try to do something you can't do; do only what you can do.

We call the technique of directing the out-of-control horse "defensive riding." The technique is not new. It's commonly used by well-grounded horsemen, and has been around for decades. Everyone I rode with as a youngster knew to direct a horse with one rein and a snaffle bit, but 75 percent of the folks I observe on the trail today don't get it.

As I write this chapter, we're retraining a 2-year-old filly. The filly came to us because a professional trainer and coach told the 13-year-old owner to sell the filly, as she was a training failure. The filly reared, ran backward and became more dangerous with each training session. Within a week, however, the filly was loping around the arena here, ears perked, pleasantly and happily doing her thing.

Why the sudden turnaround? Two things have changed. First, we ride her with a mild

You must earn and nurture your horse's trust or you could easily lose it.

snaffle and use direct-reining, or defensive-riding techniques. Second, we're teaching her to confidently go forward without trying to drag her into collection or control her with two reins just as she gets going. In other words, we're treating her like a 2-year-old filly, one that's just getting started.

Truth or Consequences

Decades of experience and thousands of horses have made it clear that the Start 'Em Right concept is diametrically opposed to the "anyone can train" concept so popularly marketed today. As our society has become more compromising and complacent about teach-

The better you understand your horse's language, the easier any task becomes.

ing self-discipline and holding individuals responsible for their actions, I'm distressed to see our youth and our horses suffering the consequences.

Interacting with horses, even minimally, by brushing, feeding or petting in a manner in which a horse's natural respect is replaced with familiarity generally causes irreversible loss of respect. "Familiarity breeds contempt" is a leadership axiom that relates equally to horsemanship. A contemptuous, 1,200-pound animal that instinctually wants to dominate to attain a higher position in the hierarchy, or just to remain in control, should cause alarm. The horse might be pleasant, interested in people and what the people are doing, and even make a rewarding pet to feed, brush and love. The common denominator is that he doesn't want to give up control to work or to become uncomfortable.

Trail work is all about giving up control and being uncomfortable. The consequences of not dealing with those two concepts aren't just potentially devastating, but inherently dangerous. Society's failure to teach horses and children to be accountable and responsible for their actions, in my opinion, is our shame. When you see an individual become self-destructive because he's confined, restrained or otherwise loses his freedom to make choices, you see an individual or animal that has learned not to accept authority.

When I was 15, I encountered my first spoiled horse. This horse had learned to make decisions about what was going to happen or not happen, and refused to accept a person as his leader. This horse flipped over backward if asked to lead when saddled, and slammed his head into a post so hard he knocked himself unconsciousness. The horse would injure himself rather than participate in training. This horse also caused me to have an arthritic leg and hip that still plague me some 40 years after I encountered him.

I never dreamed that decades later, as a gray-headed trainer, I'd have accumulated an arsenal of knowledge to deal with such a horse. I've since learned that some horses love to be fed, love to be petted, even love to have people crawl on them, but can violently react if they lose control to a wimpy human. This is not the behavior that I ever desired.

Several years ago, our local veterinarian, Tommy Martin, DVM, of Honea Path Animal Clinic, recognized that we handled horses differently than anyone he'd observed. He asked us to start clinics to help avoid injuries to horses from uninformed "trainers," as well as to avoid injuries to owners, farriers and veterinarians from abusive, spoiled horses. Today, we call those clinics "Truth or Consequences." Many of these techniques are presented in the following chapters.

Trail training starts the moment a foal is born. Set the stage for success by using these foundation-training routines.

3

MAKING A TRAIL HORSE

In years past, horses that didn't make the cut in other disciplines became trail horses. While many great trail horses come from other training programs, I've made it my mission to use my father's Start 'Em Right principles to produce and train safe, respectful and willing horses specifically for trail or recreational riding.

Genetics and training are two important factors in making a trail horse. Developing a trail horse's potential starts at birth and continues for the rest of the horse's life. You can have a well-bred horse, but if you inadvertently teach him to be unpleasant, uncooperative and unwilling to listen, or you resort to abusive techniques, you don't develop his full potential. If you resort to familiarity and lose the horse's natural respect, you deal with a disrespectful horse that, like a spoiled child, always looks for the easy way instead of the right way.

In this chapter I discuss my preferences for a trail-horse prospect, as well as offer a glimpse into my foundation-training program, which promotes confidence and respect in young horses before they're exposed to riding. This book isn't intended as a colt-starting manual, but I want you to understand how important it is to establish respect from your horse at an early age. The more quality work you do with a horse as a youngster, the less chance that you or he will be hurt when riding along the trail. The more poor training you do, the more baggage you haul down the trail.

Genetic Roulette

Selecting a trail-horse prospect begins with breeding and bloodlines. Gambling that a horse works out based on his pedigree has risks, but wagering that a horse works out without any knowledge of pedigree is a significantly bigger chance. Researching similarly bred offspring that have performed successfully in a particular discipline might offer some indications of your expectations.

Several friends and family members still ride mounts by my first Paint Horse stallion, Al's Dixon. He typically passed good minds, speed and athleticism along to his progeny. I've also had good luck raising foundation-bred stock horses, using the bloodlines prominent on large cattle ranches in the West. Generally, working ranch cowboys have no time for bloodlines that produce quirky-minded mounts.

Show records and pedigrees don't always equate to a horse the recreational rider wants or needs, but there are bloodlines known for producing reining or working cow horses that might seem great for producing trail horses. Before you make any decisions, look behind the arena and see how those horses act tied to a trailer, or while being saddled or warmed up. While observing the horses, recognize the difference between genetic dispositions and learned attitudes. In the wrong hands, a horse with excellent trail potential can act like a rogue, or a genetic time bomb can be an arena champion.

When breeding for a trail prospect, I like for both the mare and stallion to have ideal conformation and dispositions. Sometimes that's not feasible, so I avoid breeding two horses that have the same shortcomings. If one is a bit long in the back, I certainly don't breed that horse to an individual that's also long-backed.

I've bred stallions that were decent to handle and okay to ride, but sired foals with willful or hateful attitudes. I recall crossing mares in the 1960s with an American Quarter Horse Association Supreme Champion standing 50 miles from our ranch. How could we go wrong? Despite the stallion's proven athletic ability, speed and conformation, he was meaner than a stepped-on rattlesnake. Crossing the stallion with some confrontational race-bred mares produced some pretty and athletic, but dangerous rascals.

Opinions vary regarding what breeds make better trail horses. Define your idea of a trail ride before attempting to define your perfect trail horse. I come from an area, and an era, when a trail ride meant miles of riding to check cows and fences. Sometimes the terrain was rough, and there was only so much time to get a job done The pace we rode was exactly what I'd find decades later in competitive trail rides. There's a reason cowboys on big ranches cover hundreds of miles aboard Quarter Horses.

No matter your breed preference, a trail horse, like any other performance horse, must be structurally sound. Any conformational weaknesses, especially in the legs and joints, put a horse at a disadvantage on the trail and predispose him to lameness. My preference is that a horse has no leg or feet defects, period. It's not fair to expect him to hustle down a long slope at a steady trot if he's cow-hocked, has overly long pasterns, knee deformities or any other structural deviations. Even structurally sound horses can develop leg and foot issues, so why start with problems?

I avoid short-legged, "bulldog" built horses for trail mounts. An excessively thick body means the body-mass-versus-cooling-surface ratio becomes an issue. Those bulldog types just can't shed the heat quickly enough in my region. That ratio is why there are more Arabian champions on the endurance circuit. Competitive trail riding, which focuses less on the fastest time and more on control, allows other breeds to excel.

I want a short-backed horse with heavy stifle muscling to power over embankments and offer steady control sliding down hills. Some riders believe longer-backed horses have softer trots than short-backed horses. I'm not ready to concede, but I'm always interested in the comfort of a horse's trot, since I, and most competitive trail riders, predominantly ride at that gait.

Some folks confuse or equate survival of the fittest with selective reproduction. If survival of the fittest had merit for producing saddle horses, the U.S. Army wouldn't have incurred the cost and effort to implement the Remount program. Likewise, the King Ranch and other notable ranches implemented serious performance-based breeding programs to produce structurally sound, good-minded horses that could travel long distances. Gimmicks don't just come in the form of tack and training devices, they also come in the form of some intriguing, but unsound, breeding practices.

Selective breeding is about producing quality and focusing on meeting an objective. Reproducing horses because one loves a horse is fairly common, but can be a foolish decision, especially given the number of neglected, unwanted horses. Seek a professional horseman's opinion before taking a chance with a breeding program based on emotion. You don't do anyone or any horse any favors by breeding horses on your emotions and sheer desire to raise a foal. Many people, before they have spoiled youngsters with dangerous behavioral issues in their backyards, fail to consider that raising horses is a huge responsibility.

Handle your foal from the moment it's born, holding it with your hands and body, as shown. Place your left hand under the foal's neck, and glide your right hand down its hind leg, just below its buttocks.

A Foal's Most Important Lesson

Once I have a structurally and genetically sound foal, then environmental factors become paramount. Often I'm asked when I start training a young trail prospect. Training begins the moment the youngster is born. An acceptable alternative is to stay away from the foal until he's ready to train, be it weeks, months or even two years, but I choose to handle a foal right away, ensuring that my training isn't a traumatic event for the animal.

I never handle a foal at a time or location that I don't have total control of the situation. For example, I never approach a foal in the pasture, and I don't want him approaching me, because doing so allows him to take control of a training session. Allowing a horse to do that, even at a young age, can have long-term ramifications, including confrontation issues.

I also don't feed my horses treats, just as I didn't give my children candy bars for cleaning their rooms or doing their homework. I expected them to do these jobs just as I expect my horses to do what I ask. Offering treats confuses a horse about when and where he's allowed to enter your space. Furthermore, feeding treats can lead to nibbling, which can degenerate into biting. I don't reward a horse unless he's earned it. Doing so can lead to familiarity in lieu of respect.

My training motivation is the long-term welfare of a horse, not what makes me feel good or what makes the horse comfortable. Similarly, not one training technique takes priority over what a horse needs to be a successful riding partner.

The most important thing all my horses learn is a kiss cue signaling them to get away from my space. It might not be the first thing they learn, but it's a foundation for life. This "get away" cue is the most important safety feature you can teach the horse, because when an accident happens, or if the horse reacts for whatever reason, you don't want him reacting or doing anything else in your space. However, don't introduce this cue until your young horse stands tied quietly, confidently allows you to halter him, accepts having his feet handled and is confident that you won't violate his trust.

Once you have some trust to go with your horse's natural respect, introduce the get-away cue in a round pen. With a respectful horse, step back quietly, raise your hands over your head and make a kissing sound. By now the horse should understand that sound means move—*now*. If the horse moves away, great; his reward is being free of your directions.

If he doesn't move, there are consequences. Depending on the horse and how easily his feelings are hurt, you can flip your halter at his ribs, kick pebbles at his legs, or, for a disrespectful horse that ignores you, flip your longe whip toward him. When he moves out of your area, you've accomplished your mission. If not, give him a smack with the whip. Your horse must understand that your space is never to be violated, and he must always remain clear of you unless you ask him to come closer. I use this philosophy and lesson consistently, which enables me to wander safely through my herd without horses fighting in my vicinity or being difficult to catch.

If a horse isn't respectful enough to move out of your space when you ask, there's a problem, and it's usually human-induced, rather than horse-induced. A horse that understands to get away when you make a kissing noise also understands how to move forward when you begin round-pen work the following year, and riding later.

On my farm, I don't allow others to feed, touch or get close to my foals unless the people understand the Start 'Em Right concept. Youngsters that come in to be fed and regularly have people within 10 feet can quickly presume to threaten, or at least lose respect for, humans. I've seen many babies develop familiarity issues before they were even haltered. Once you lose a foal's natural respect, it takes a long time to re-establish it, if it's ever re-established.

Handling a Foal

Initially, I handle a foal without a halter, restraining him with my hands and body. During the first few days of a foal's life, I touch the youngster all over his body. To do this with your foal, hold the baby with your left hand under his neck and your right hand just below where the tail begins. Hold the foal gently but firmly. If you aren't willing to bang around like a backyard football, leave the foal handling to someone who is. If you grab and grab, and lose the foal and lose the foal, you teach him not only to run from you, but also to attempt to out-muscle you. Try to get your hands on the foal with as little excitement as possible, while staying on your feet and not turning loose. As long as you remember that the foal's training is more important than your broken toe, bruised shin or manicured nails, you can hold on to him.

As you rub the foal, watch for touchy areas. Youngsters are particularly sensitive between the front legs and the flanks, as well as between the rear legs. Prey animals typically grab and hold these areas until they subdue their prey. If a foal doesn't like having his ears rubbed, rub them, move away, and then come back. Move your hands somewhere else, and then back to the ears. During this initial training, also pick up the foal's feet and hold each until he quits jerking, then put down the foot. Rarely is it a good idea to punish a foal at this stage unless you're forced to correct some other human's attempt at training.

Repeat this process anywhere from five to 15 minutes each time you handle the foal for the first few days. If he objects to being handled anywhere, that's where you should focus. The youngster, or any horse, shouldn't have the option of making decisions in your training program.

Recognizing that each horse is an individual, try to introduce different techniques at different times. For example, if you have a youngster that runs away, introduce him to the halter and lead next. He quickly learns that his runaway mode results in firm direction from the lead.

All our foals need to learn to face their handlers, in spite of being frightened. At no time does a foal have the luxury of aiming his rear toward me or placing a foot on me. Discipline at this age is seldom needed or used, and foals that need disciplining for kicking and biting are rare and unfortunate. I immediately consider eliminating mares or stallions from my breeding program if I encounter such problems with their progeny.

Square-Pen Training

Relaxed foals are likely to be introduced to square-pen training before haltering. In this exercise, a foal learns to keep his rear end turned away from his handler.

Square-pen training is based on the same horse psychology as round-pen training (See Chapter 4, "Round-Pen Reasoning."), but requires more finesse, attention to detail and knowledge of horse psychology than many handlers have. I first saw my dad do square-pen training in the late 1950s, and it started

Rub the foal's entire body with one hand and pick up each leg, still holding the foal with your other hand. Hold each foot until the foal stops trying to jerk it away.

Rub the foal's lips and gums, and stick your fingers in the corners of his mouth, which prepares him for bitting.

If the foal ignores your "kiss" cue or turns his hind end toward you, deliver a firm and deliberate tap on the hip with a longe whip to get his attention.

Repeat the kiss-tap sequence until the baby acknowledges you with both eyes. Then turn away from him to reward him.

me on my path toward what's now called "natural horsemanship."

The corners in a square pen help prevent a foal from just running around, which defeats the purpose of your training. You can back into a corner to block a running foal. Or, you can push the foal into a corner and insist that he turn and face you. The corners help block the foal from making decisions that would allow him to run. The ultimate goals for a trail horse are for him to face up to danger and not run away, to look to his rider for leadership and respond willingly, and to spook in place. The square pen provides a foundation for all of these things.

Square-pen training encourages a horse to look at you with both eyes—a sign of respect. First, make a kissing sound, encouraging the horse to look at you. If he doesn't respond, follow the kiss with a tap on the hip, using a longe whip with no tail. Repeat the kiss-tap sequence until the foal looks at you. When the baby looks at you with both eyes, turn your body 180 to 270 degrees away from him, removing the confrontation and rewarding him.

When the youngster looks away again, kiss to him. If he gives you his attention, reward him with relaxation. If not, begin tapping his hip again. Move slowly and methodically to avoid spooking the youngster. Remember, horses are much more attentive to body language than people are because that's the horses' natural language. People who are naturally jerky in their movements achieve limited success with horses until the humans learn to control their "noisy" mannerisms. Too much or overly harsh pressure instills fright in the foal. Using too little pressure or being too tentative just annoys the foal and teaches him to be irritated to the point of kicking or resisting.

Try to limit your square-pen training to 5-minute sessions to keep the baby's attention, but don't quit until you have at least one successful look. With consistency and attention to detail, the youngster can join up and stand next to you just as an older, respectful horse in a round pen does. Eventually, the baby learns to follow you around the square pen.

Once the youngster learns to face, and then stand next to a handler, you can start moving away. If the baby breaks away, begin the slow, methodical kissing-tapping routine again. Reward success by turning out the youngster with his mom.

Halter Training

Begin halter training in the square pen. I use hand-tied rope halters with tied leads, rather than snaps. I don't need any metal objects flopping around banging my babies. I recently tried some halters with $^3/8$-inch nylon, which has more spring and less abra-

As you halter your foal for the first time, maneuver him into a corner and stand beside him, using your body and the fence as barriers if he wants to move away.

Stand in front of your foal and gently tug to one side on the rope.

Your tugging signals him to unweight a foot and step forward to release the pressure.

sion when a foal decides to throw a tantrum, but ¼-inch diameter also works well.

If you successfully have completed the training described above, haltering isn't an issue. If you need to halter an out-of-control foal, begin just like you did handling a foal for the first time. Once the foal stands quietly, maneuver him against or almost against a panel. Then slide the long crown part of the halter, which eventually goes over his poll, under his throat with your left hand, and reach over his neck with your right arm to take the long portion in that hand. If the foal wants to dance around, use your body to press him against the panels. The foal can't go forward because you have the halter under his neck and in each hand. With your left hand on the noseband and your right hand on the long crown piece, slide the noseband up and over the foal's nose, without excessively rubbing against the hair. Then fasten the halter.

Once the youngster is haltered, begin teaching him to lead. Move ahead of him and gently tug on the lead, cueing him to step forward. This tug should be to the side, not to the front, to encourage the baby to shift his weight off one leg and take a step sideways. When you get that response, rub the foal's shoulder, which is a signal to relax, not a reward; relaxing is the reward.

Pulling on the rope encourages your foal to brace against the pressure. Instead, flex his neck with the lead, kiss to him and drive him forward from the hip.

If necessary, tug quickly and deliberately on the rope to launch the foal forward, which teaches him that your cues mean "go forward now."

If necessary, for a stubborn baby, stand six feet in front of the youngster, cue with a small tug, then intensify the tug, launching the baby toward you. As soon as the youngster is close, rub his shoulder. The key to this technique is not to pull the baby—just cue, then launch. You don't want an argument, just compliance to a cue, and to give the reward.

How fast you work depends on the foal's temperment. If he's volatile or hyper, allow plenty of time between cues and rewards. If the baby is easily distracted, keep your training session moving so he doesn't lose interest.

At the end of your leading session, unhalter the youngster, but be careful not to do anything that encourages him to run away. Remove the halter and move away from him quietly but quickly. You want him always to understand that he doesn't get away at this point—instead, you allow him his freedom.

Ready for the Road

My foal's first trailer ride is generally in a stock trailer. I want a baby to ride next to his dam, so I prefer a large door opening. I also like a stock trailer because it lets in more light than many horse trailers, which makes the enclosure less intimidating to the baby.

Park your trailer so the wheels have just dropped off a high area. The closer the trailer floor is to the ground, the easier to get the baby on the trailer. Avoid loading a baby near a busy highway, near barbed wire fences or any other dangerous place. If possible, load the youngster in a pasture. Consider having four portable panels connected and nearby so you can slide the baby into a partial pen with the only exit being into the trailer. Avoid approaching this training with an attitude that you're going to teach the baby to get into the

Your foal should lead willingly before you attempt to load him in the trailer, which can seem like a scary black hole to your horse.

trailer. Your first priority is to assure any baby that the trailer is nothing to fear.

Have a helper lead the foal's dam to the trailer, stopping with the mare's front feet just short of stepping into it. Then position the baby either between your hip and the dam's left hip, or, if the baby doesn't lead well, wrap your arms around his body as described earlier, keeping his face close to the dam's flank.

When you're in position, ask your helper to load the mare as steadily and slowly as possible. Step with your right foot between the baby's rear feet, your knee against the lower buttocks or hind legs, your right hand on the hip, and your left hand on the side of the neck, just behind the ears. As the dam loads, keep pushing the baby against the mare. You might need one hard push to keep the baby loading with the dam.

Repeat this process each time you load while the baby is less than a month old. Two or three times following the dam into the trailer with you bumping and pushing, and the baby soon gets in the trailer. By the time a baby is a month old, his leading skills should be honed to the point you can lead him into the trailer.

Whatever you do, avoid pulling and coaxing to get a foal in the trailer. That only develops resistance and is an example of why I so often tell folks, "We don't teach our babies to load; we just avoid teaching them not to load!" There is a difference.

Instead of pulling on the rope, forcing the horse to load, cue him to move forward with lead-rope pressure or walk toward the horse's hip with a loose lead. Reinforce your body language with a verbal kiss cue. If the youngster doesn't comply, you can swat his

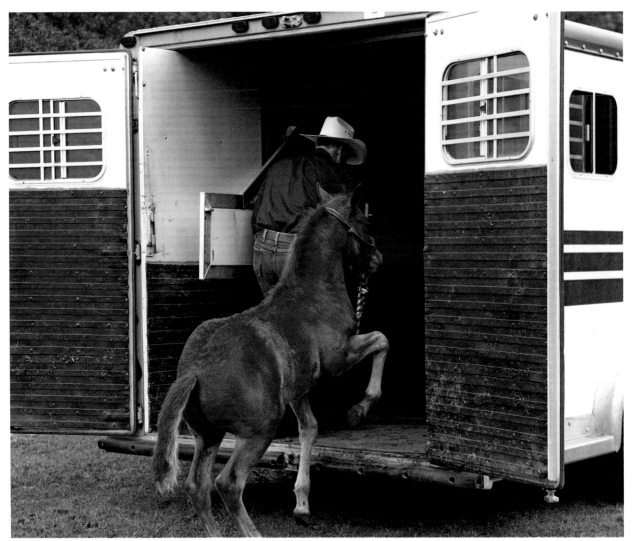

Your first goal in trailer-loading: Assure your horse that the trailer is nothing to fear, which requires leading him inside without coaxing or pulling.

Once inside the trailer, your youngster might not want to leave, because it's his security. Apply gentle sideways pressure on the lead rope, as you did when leading him forward, so he unweights a foot and steps—or, most likely—jumps from the trailer.

hip with a longe whip. That little sting should be quick and deliberate, so your horse understands that when you kiss, he should move right away. Repeat this a few times, and the youngster figures out that it's more comfortable to load into the trailer than to continue practicing the "cue, kiss, move or get a smack" sequence. Remember, however, that the trailer is not the place to introduce the kiss cue. Your youngster should understand that cue before you progress to trailer-loading.

Yearling Training

Once our young horses receive this initial training, we turn them out to be horses until they're yearlings. During that year, once every 30 to 60 days, they still get their hooves and bridle paths trimmed and are dewormed. If one that needs more training catches our attention, we bring him into a round pen or catch pen for daily refresher courses for three to seven days. Once the youngster shows willingness and attentiveness to the handler, he goes back to the pasture.

As yearlings, the horses are saddled and bridled for the first time. Introduce your horse to the saddle in a safe enclosure, such as the round pen or breeding stocks. Tie the horse using the tips outlined in Chapter 5, "Never a Fit to be Tied," and set the saddle and blanket about 10 feet from him, in a spot he can see and become familiar with them. When your horse isn't fazed by the presence of the gear, gradually move it closer to him, eventually sacking him out with the blanket and saddle, respectively, as explained in Chapter 6, "Simple Sack-Out."

When your horse remains calm, with the saddle and blanket touching him, move him to a 12-by-12-foot pen for bridling. Remove the reins for the initial bridling session so they don't get in the way or spook the youngster.

Don't get in a hurry or become excited when bridling, just quietly slide the bridle into place. Some riders want to get the bridle on in one quick step. That just excites the horse and triggers confrontation. Instead, remove the halter, placing your right hand over the horse's neck, passing the bridle under his neck to your right hand. Then slowly draw your right wrist onto his poll, while steadying the bit with your left hand. When your right wrist is on the poll, slide your wrist forward, open the bridle with your left hand and slide the bridle over the nose.

If the horse moves around, leave your hands where they are until he quits moving, then continue with the training. Next, bring the bit under his chin with your left hand. When he stands quietly, move your right wrist back on his poll, while using your left-hand fingers to guide the bit to his lips. At that point, press the thumb on your left hand to the left corner of his mouth. Pause for a moment, then slide your thumb between his lips at the corner of his mouth, and wait a second before sliding your thumb onto his gum, between his teeth.

If he starts working his mouth, use the fingers on your left hand to slide the bit between his teeth, but without touching his teeth. Your right wrist has moved back of the poll so, even if he moves around, the bridle

Prior to saddling your horse for the first time, sack him out with the blanket and saddle, so he's not afraid of them.

When saddling your horse, keep your elbow against his side, as shown, so you can push yourself away if he suddenly blows up.

A round pen or breeding stocks are safe places to saddle a horse for the first time.

is still in place. You might eventually have to press your thumb on his gums, but a normal, respectful yearling by this time is "gumming" and accepts the bit, hoping to get rid of your thumb. Replace the halter over the bridle, and take the yearling to the round pen for his first saddling.

Tie your horse to the pen, using the guidelines in Chapter 5, "Never a Fit to be Tied." Slowly place the blanket and saddle on his back, and quickly and quietly snug the front cinch just enough that the saddle stays on the horse. Then buckle the rear cinch and breast collar. The horse might try bucking and running, but if he's tied to the rail, he can't do much. If you've progressed through the previous foundation-training sequences, there aren't any tantrums or flailing around on the ground. If such behavior arises, back off and let it happen.

I generally leave my youngsters saddled and tied 30 to 45 minutes. I really don't want to see them bucking and running around in fear, because that's counterproductive to my training program. Thirty to 45 minutes after the last of any bucking or blowups, you can release the lead rope and move out of the way, in case your horse runs and starts bucking. Allow the yearling to move around for 30 minutes so he becomes accustomed to the stirrups bumping his sides, the saddle's weight, etc. That's enough for one session.

During the second saddling, advance to bitting your horse. This procedure teaches a youngster to give to the rein pulling on the bit, and it's part of teaching the horse to take guidance from the rein in preparation for his first ride as a 2-year-old.

It's important to follow logic when bitting a horse, because it can be dangerous if done incorrectly. Tie the rein to the rear saddle dee, to the point your horse's neck flexes to the side no more than 15 degrees. Once you tie the rein to the saddle, place your hand on your horse's nose and gently bring it around to the snap on the rein. Then quickly move away. Occasionally a hot-blooded youngster can be greatly offended and throw a tantrum. Most try to feel their way out of the pressure.

Once you can saddle and bridle your horse, bit him up so he learns to yield to direct-rein pressure, an exercise that carries over when you start riding him.

Fifteen to 20 minutes after you see a youngster giving to the rein, bit him up in the same manner on the other side. This is when the youngster is most likely to throw a tantrum. He just spent 15 to 20 minutes learning to give to the left when he felt a pull on the bit, and now the rein is pulling to the right, but he must try to solve the issue by going left. Once he gives to the bit for 15 to 20 minutes, give him the rest of the day off.

The next session, repeat the entire bitting-up procedure, gradually working up to flexing his neck 30 degrees, but never more than that. Once the horse accepts the saddle and bridle, he's ready for ground-driving with the saddle and bridle. Refer to Chapter 7 for ground-driving instructions.

From there, you're ready to begin his initial saddle training, which is beyond the scope of this book. But, because there are several good colt-starting books and articles available, we've dedicated the majority of this book to solving common problems riders encounter on the trail with horses that weren't started right or have been allowed too many liberties throughout their training.

Learn how round-pen training is different from simply training in a round pen with this fundamental wisdom.

4

ROUND-PEN REASONING

Trail riders, like riders in other disciplines, should safely get their horses' attention and respect before loading them in a trailer or climbing on their backs. Done properly, round-pen training is the safest, most time-efficient way to make the mental adjustment necessary to complete these tasks. If I have a trail horse that's energetic to the point of being rowdy, a timid horse or a horse that lacks respect for me, doing round-pen training before I haul, saddle or ride him can reduce the chances of him or me getting hurt.

Some people and clinicians use round pens as entertainment, and some use their pens to simply tire their horses. I use the round pen as a training tool.

Round-pen training capitalizes on a horse's instinctual tendencies to be a follower by supplanting the lead mare with the trainer. The result can be that a horse "joins" you, respecting you as the head of the herd and willingly following your lead.

If you're like the majority of the recreational-riding population, you probably feel as though you're too old to get bucked off; me, too. That's one reason I incorporate a round pen into my training program. I want a horse to agree to cooperate before I get on his back. I like to ask the horse to do things in his language, and the round pen is a great place to learn that form of communication. If he says no, I can continue my groundwork and saddle training until he's ready to cooperate.

When working a client's horse, I use round-pen training with the owner present during the first lesson or two. I want the owner to see how the horse communicates his fear, irritation or anger at being directed by me, the "lead mare." I use the training as a diagnostic tool and am generally able to predict how a horse will respond to training and how far I can get in 30, 60 or 90 days by briefly working him in the round pen and seeing how he reacts. I adjust my approach with each horse,

Standing with her front legs wide and head up, the mare doesn't show respectful, submissive body language. I walk to her left side with my whip out, directing her to move away from the whip and my arm. My directive is firm and unequivocal.

depending on what he tells me. I also can detect horses that are prone to "renegotiate" how much they're willing to cooperate.

Before you can use a round pen correctly, you first must understand three things:

1) Why it works: Consider the lead mare versus follower relationship, as well as intimidation versus intimidated.

2) How it works: Use a horse's body language to understand the horse.

3) How to make it work: Use your body language to influence the horse.

In this chapter, I explain these critical elements so you can learn to use a round pen safely and effectively. First, however, let's discuss the type of pen most suitable for my round-pen training.

Round-Pen Sizes

Round pens come in various sizes. I prefer a 65-foot pen. I find I'm not able to influence the horse enough in a 75-foot pen, and a 50-foot pen is too small for the horse to relax as he moves away. In my experience, however, you have to find what works for your size and demeanor. Cattle panels work for quiet, calm horses but keep in mind that if a horse can stick his head above a 5-foot panel, his body is likely to try to follow.

I can't count the number of cattle panels I have seen crushed by horses getting irritated and deciding to depart the training area. The horse typically does not sustain damage, but has now learned, when frustrated, to heck with cooperating—just charge through the panel fencing.

Real round-pen panels are 6 feet high and tend to be heavier duty than cattle panels. Most cattle panels have S-shaped center uprights. These work okay for counter-clockwise work, but take chunks out of knees, ankles or hooves if a horse bumps against the panels going clockwise.

Why it Works

A person can most easily understand why round-pen training works by spending a few years observing equine interaction within a herd. However, few people have the time and resources to do that. Watching stalled horses turned out for a daily romp doesn't count. That's more like having time in the exercise yard at a prison than watching horses interact in their natural environment. There are herds

The mare doesn't respond to my directive, so I bend my knees, ready to spring at her in an assertive manner, like a lead mare. If this mare allows her body to remain fixed, she knows she'll get a flick of the whip.

The mare's elevated head and neck indicate energy to the point of being playful. However, she has an ear pointed toward me, indicating she's watching and listening, and her arced body tells me she's interested in cooperating, rather than escaping.

of pastured horses to watch, though, if you look for them.

In a herd setting, if a lead mare steps toward a choice clump of tender grass, the subordinate horses move away. If she heads toward water or better grass, they follow her. If a new horse is allowed to join the band, he can elect to join the rest of the herd and follow the lead mare or can challenge the lead mare for the helm. No voting, consensus or "I'm okay, you're okay" attitude. Challenging the lead mare, or even failing to submit to her, can result in a full-grown horse down for the count.

A visitor to my farm once watched a lead mare and her buddy kept in a large pen together. When the lead mare decided she wanted more space, things became ugly. In 30 seconds or so, the other horse was down and in shock. I suspect if we'd not been present, there could've been a death. To the casual observer, it might've appeared we were watching one nasty mare. But we were, in fact, watching one lead mare.

A lead mare's behavior is instinctual and based on intimidation. Some people consider "intimidation" an ugly word, but it's part of the natural horse-herd dynamics. If you want to understand and use round-pen training effectively, you must supplant the intimidating lead mare. If you act like a wimp, the horses treat you with a lack of respect, not as the lead horse.

Let's talk briefly about what round-pen training is not. I work closely with a veterinarian near my home, which is how I started doing clinics. He was concerned about people abusing horses during round-pen training. These so-called "trainers" often used deep sand in their pens or weighted the horses with hundreds of pounds. In my program, using exhaustion to "train" a horse is not an option,

This is flowing animation. I move quickly, but not aggressively, to motivate the mare. Although not entirely relaxed, she's not fearful. Her ears show that she's not intimidated, and she moves with a slightly raised head and neck and animation, which tell me she's trying to cooperate.

nor is using the round pen for entertainment purposes. The pen is for real training.

How it Works

As described in the last section, the lead mare and her herd communicate with body language. Learning to read that body language is akin to learning a foreign language— it takes time and study, and not everyone has equal abilities. We train a couple of interns each summer, plus students in my Train the Trainer program. Some pick up on equine body language easily, and other just get frustrated. I can't teach you Spanish in one book, nor can I teach you the equine language in one book. So I assume your comprehension of horse language is pretty good from your time spent working with horses.

You can see the translation from the herd leader to the human "horse" leader in the round pen by monitoring your horse's attentiveness, cooperation, respect, or lack thereof. As you enter the round pen, your horse should address you with at least one eye. You can tell where the horse's attention is by watching his ears. If he doesn't have an ear focused on you, then his body language is demonstrating that he's not focused on you.

If your horse doesn't move away when you kiss and raise your arms, he's demonstrating poor training or uncooperativeness. If he kicks at you or threatens to kick by pinning his ears, he's telling you he feels he has the right to punish you, as evidenced by his disrespect. If he moves around the pen, he might appear to be cooperative. But if he looks outside the pen, his body language demonstrates that he's not interested in cooperation.

When asked to turn, a horse turning away from you looks for a way out, not to cooperate with you. If he pins his ears, he shows

My body language is relaxed as I move. The mare's ears and face show she's attentive and moving with me without fear, intimidation or playfulness.

aggressive defiance. When you ask him to turn and he maintains constant speed, that could be a sign he's not paying attention. The horse that speeds up and attempts to charge past you is expressing frustration, or contempt. Determining if that frustration is from fear or a lack of respect is usually apparent from earlier body language.

Making it Work

Once I put a horse in the round pen, I ask him to go. Years ago, I clucked to the horse to get movement, but today I find I can vary the intensity and length of a kiss noise easier than a cluck.

Place your body between the center of the pen and the horse's hip. If you're oriented too forward, your body position signals your horse to turn. If you're too far back, he doesn't understand that you seriously want him to move forward.

If a horse cuts across the pen, walk toward his ribs, moving him back to the edge of the pen. You must watch the horse, as well as anticipate and interpret his movement and language constantly. Look for the horse to start giving you his inside ear, indicating that he's paying attention. If he looks outside, he's thinking about going outside. Occasionally, a horse turns his head to look outside but has an ear tilted toward you. That's a sign you have a horse that understands what you want, but is trying to play things cool.

Make sure your horse learns to go and pay attention before you do any serious turning. For horses raised at my farm, that might be five laps in each direction. Those raised to think they're humans might take five or more lessons to readily move ahead.

Without an expert being there to interpret, watch and assist, most people don't recognize when a horse is moving and cooperating, or just moving because the person is making him move. That's a subtle but important difference. If you want to get the most training value for your time, you must master this body language.

Extremes vary from a horse tearing around the pen, which indicates you might be acting too confrontational or intimidating, to a horse

Here's an image of respectful cooperation. This mare is somewhat relaxed and attentive to me with her eyes and ears, and follows me as I walk and drop the whip.

Even though the mare allows me to rub her face and appears relaxed, her neck is elevated. These mixed signals tell me the mare is tolerating the petting, but not respectfully submitting.

The mare appears relaxed and obedient, but both ears are pointed forward, which indicates she's not focused on me. This tells me the mare is a bit more familiar with the routine than I like and could quickly take advantage of the situation.

that doesn't move or even kicks at you because you aren't being confrontational enough. Don't teach the horse not to go. Don't teach him to ignore your verbal cues, your kisses. Sometimes I see people repeatedly kiss to their horses but without reinforcing the cue with human body language and the rope or whip. It's just like teaching a student to ride: kiss, squeeze and kick. In this case it's kiss, confront and push with the rope or whip.

Once you have a serviceable round pen and recognize these basics, you can start working on transitions and directional changes, using the pen to further your horse's training and responsiveness, not just to wear him out. A little work goes a long way in the round pen, so divide your sessions into 15- to 30-minute intervals so your horse doesn't become sour. As your power of observation and ability to interpret equine body language improve, your sessions become smoother and more productive. Your horse will start to follow your lead—a sign of a respectful partner.

5
NEVER A FIT
TO BE TIED

Y ou're on a scenic ride and stop to take a look at a water-
fall. You undo your lead rope and tie your horse to a
nearby tree. The next thing you know, your horse has
moved around so much he's become tangled and starts to pull
back in panic toward a drop-off.

Standing tied is one of the most important skills a trail horse
learns. You never know when you'll need to tie him in an emergency or during an overnight trail ride. But if he doesn't stand
still or he pulls back, that's a sign that you've forgotten a step in
his foundation training. That oversight could become dangerous.

Having a horse that doesn't stand still when tied is like having
a child that doesn't stay in a seat belt. Occasionally there are
critical and dangerous times we need to count on that child or
that horse remaining in place while we handle some emergency.

When tying horses I prefer using halters and leads with no metal hardware or gadgets that could break, injure a horse or create other problems.

If your horse, or your child, needs constant baby-sitting, you've failed to provide an environment that allows him to grow to be a responsible, accountable individual. A person who's guilty of not providing an appropriate environment for his horse to become responsible and accountable, most likely has other deficit areas besides tying.

In this chapter, I offer tips to safely introduce your horse to being tied. This is such an important skill that we start teaching our horses to stand tied as foals, as you can see from the photographs. A foal is less powerful and less likely to get hurt or to injure you. Even though I show the techniques on a foal, the techniques apply to horses of all ages. Keep in mind, the first couple of times you tie your horse might be ugly, but it doesn't have to be unsafe, and you shouldn't ignore teaching your horse to tie. Some things don't get better with age.

When teaching your horse to tie, always carry a pocketknife or multipurpose tool in case you need to cut the rope in an emergency. Also remain nearby in case a real emergency, not to be mistaken for a tantrum, arises, as well as to assess the next appropriate training step, based on your horse's actions and reactions.

The Restraint Debate

The last 20 years, I've seen a rash of horses that don't stand to be tied. I believe our culture has been seduced by the theory that it's easier to make excuses than to train properly. Some justify their excuses, saying, "I want to avoid neck injuries in my horse. In the last decade, there have been several claims about the purported danger of tying horses." My calls to veterinary clinics in the area confirm my 50 years of experience: There's no reason you shouldn't tie your horse.

A veterinarian with more than 30 years experience in our rural area, which has the highest equine density in South Carolina, stated he'd never seen a horse with a neck injury from tying. Another veterinarian, with 40 years of large-animal experience, primarily horses, said he'd seen a few neck injuries, but couldn't confirm that tying caused any. Furthermore, he added that he's seen head injuries from owners and trainers tying with breakaway equipment. This particular equine veterinarian specifically spoke of breakaway equipment to include poor quality snaps and halters and inadequate tie racks, as well as intentional breakaway equipment. He further discussed folks who tied with strings and other gimmicks that allowed a horse to flip over backward when inadequately tied. I find it disappointing that people cause damage to their horses by substituting gimmicks in lieu of good training.

The latter veterinarian runs an operation that raises Quarter Horses and averages more than a dozen foals each year. They don't imprint the babies, but choose instead to handle the babies when weaning. Within three training sessions, their babies stand tied. As with our 75-year-old operation, the owner-trainer stated that in more than a half-century he's never had a neck injury from tying a horse. I think the conclusion is obvious.

Tying Tips

Tip 1: Tie to a sturdy post. Find something solid to which you can tie your horse. A post buried two feet deep is not solid, even if it's anchored in concrete. I set a post 3½ feet to 4 feet in the ground, so it's stable, and I don't like posts less than 8 inches in diameter.

In the round pen, avoid tying near the corner of panels. If a horse launches himself onto the panels, you don't want a front foot to become hung where the panels connect near the top. It's better to tie to the top of a panel and in the middle of a 6-foot-tall panel. Don't tie to panels unless they're supported at either end by posts or by panels connected perpendicularly, and never tie to cattle panels. A horse can bend them, and the panels have curved top corners that funnel a horse's leg between the rails. Dragging a panel, or anything, frightens a horse, so if it's possible to move the object to which you're tying your horse, reconsider and tie to a safer option.

When I first tie a foal, I desensitize it with gentle sacking out (covered in the next chapter), so the baby feels the pull on the end of the rope. This filly's response shows that she's thinking and willing to learn.

When she feels the initial pressure, the filly pulls back, the reaction I want. She eventually associates the pressure with her, not me, pulling on the rope, and learns that when she yields to the pressure, it releases.

Tie rings on most modern trailers are inadequate. The cast-aluminum rings can be broken or pulled loose by a determined, small adult horse. I've added steel tie rings above the factory-produced ties on my aluminum trailer. I might tie a weanling to an aluminum ring, but I tie yearlings and older horses to the steel rings. On my stock trailers, I tie to the uprights, above a horse's eye level.

I don't tie a horse to crossties until he's riding well. If he throws a tantrum in crossties, he might question the authority of being tied. Many of our youngsters most likely could stand in crossties without incident. The chance that tying in crossties could become a training incident is lessened as a horse progresses through training.

On the trail, I'm very careful when tying a young horse to an overhead line. The flopping line can frighten a horse into pulling back. If I question the line's strength, I don't tie a horse to it. Likewise, if I question a tie rack's construction, I don't tie to it. It's better to be inconvenienced for 10 minutes and hold a horse, than to be inconvenienced for the rest of the horse's life as he tests every other tying situation.

Tip 2: Use strong equipment. Outfit your horse in a halter and lead rope that are just as durable as they are practical. I prefer hand-tied halters of $5/16$-inch diameter braided nylon or nylon-polypropylene material. The $5/16$-inch diameter adds about 50 percent more strength over the ¼-inch material. Furthermore, the $5/16$-inch appears to be less abrasive than the ¼-inch. I don't use flat nylon halters anymore. The quality of the hardware has become difficult to discern. I don't want to guess about quality in my training equations. My lead ropes are made of the same material as the halter and in at least $9/16$-inch to $5/8$-inch diameter. Smaller diameter ropes typically lack both strength and wearability, plus they're hard to hold.

Tip 3: Tie high and tight. Tie your horse even with or, even better, above his eye level, leaving the lead rope just long enough that he can relax and sleep. Tying in this manner prevents him from engaging his front end if he pulls back, as well as keeps him from ducking his head under the lead and pulling the halter over his ears.

There are several knots you can use to tie a hors, but I rely on a standard quick-release knot for convenience and safety. If you tie high and to something solid, as I describe above, there's no reason you need a quick-release. My daughter, Jennifer, uses a bowline knot, especially on horses that might untie themselves.

Philosophically, if you tie your horse so he can get loose, he learns to get loose and continues to expect to get loose the rest of his life. However, if you tie your horse so he doesn't get loose, he learns not to get loose and doesn't try to get loose. Not understanding this simple concept is the root of confusion for so many people and their horses. You either create the situation for successfully tying your horse, or you create the problem, which has no good solution.

Tip 4: Don't give in to tantrums or gimmicks. If your horse throws a tantrum, don't release him. Rewarding the tantrum only teaches him that tantrums are alternatives, which creates dangerous training challenges later in life. If you feel a need to run and untie the horse, remember that you endanger yourself and are responsible for rewarding a horse for something that you really don't want him to learn. Generally, a horse that throws a tantrum and flops on the ground doesn't need help getting up. Let him be uncomfortable,

Here the foal fights the pressure. I allow her to do so, even if she falls on the ground, until...

...she realizes that she controls the pressure and decides it's much easier to stand than resist the pressure.

I tie a horse in the panel's center, where my lead stays secure, and above the horse's eye level so he doesn't get tangled in the rope. I also remain in the vicinity to monitor my horse and carry a multipurpose tool in case I need it.

thrash around and finish throwing his tantrum. Then let him get back on his feet. This is no more dangerous than a child throwing a tantrum when he doesn't get the candy bar he thinks he deserves. Give in, and you're always giving in to the tantrum.

Likewise, I want an immediate reward when the horse yields to the lead. This doesn't happen if he's tied to a bungee, inner tube or gimmick. One party motivated to not see a horse uncomfortable, plus another party motivated to profit from selling gimmicks, equals a lifelong hazardous horse.

I don't use gimmicks that allow lead ropes to slide or stretch. The idea might sound effective to an overprotective owner, but being overprotective is just as counterproductive as being abusive, and much more common. I want a horse to feel the immediate consequence of pulling back. I don't believe in letting a rope slide, or using a bungee or inner tube. These allow the horse to decide how far he pulls. These gimmicks don't teach the horse to stop pulling back.

Should the gimmick fail, or the handler fail to manage the gimmick, the horse gets a lesson about getting loose. I want an immediate consequence because the horse can understand a well-defined and immediate consequence. Keep in mind that gimmicks can increase the chance of your horse flipping over and injuring his head. If you want a solid trail horse, a team player and not just a volunteer who decides when to cooperate or to rebel, start your horse right, without gadgets.

Problem-Solving Strategies

I see three common disrespectful behaviors in tied horses: pawing, chewing on leads and poking their heads into things. These actions indicate that a horse feels free to express his dissatisfaction, frustration and boredom. The symptoms were seldom problems 50 years ago, and they're not problems in many of today's hard-working ranch horses. Actually, these actions aren't really problems at all, but rather symptoms of another problem many horse owners don't understand or refuse to accept: They've lost their horses' respect or have traded it for familiarity.

To explain my point another way, think of a group of high-school boys the first morning of football camp, waiting for the head coach. They're joking, having fun, and just being boys. Fast forward to the last day of football camp. Same setting, same boys, but this time they're quietly talking, not goofing around or joking. The difference is respect. Through the course of the season, they've learned to keep their heads down, do their jobs and not draw attention to themselves. They ask questions if needed, pay attention and respect the coach or reap the consequences. Those who demand respect get it; those who don't get little.

If you lose your horse's respect, you can regain it only one session at a time, and some days that respect might carry over to the next, but other days you must start over. The hardest thing for people to understand: Horses are too precious for people to abdicate their responsibility and instead try to build a bond based on love. That's unfair to a horse.

So, if you have a pawer, chewer or fidgeter, I recommend two training avenues: either correct the action or set up the horse for success. To correct the action, you need to consistently be aware of what your horse is doing while he's tied and be ready to take action. Stand where you're not obvious to the horse and throw a piece of gravel at him when he starts chewing, pawing or disobeying.

I prefer to avoid putting a horse in a situation where I must correct him. That's why I like to tie my horses as foals, allowing them to get accustomed to the pressure and experience the consequences of not yielding to the restriction while they're smaller and less dangerous. If I do see a youngster expressing signs of boredom or frustration, I put him to work, teaching him to pick up his feet, accept sacking out, anything to keep his mind occupied until he's ready to stand quietly and be left alone. This sounds like a simple concept, but it takes imagination and dedication on your part to implement. The rewards are major, though, for both you and your horse.

Control your horse's urge to spook with this sack-out technique.

6

A SIMPLE SACK-OUT

Sacking out your horse, or rubbing objects over his entire body, introduces him to sensations he'll experience on the trail—or anywhere. It builds his confidence, reducing his natural flight-or-fight reaction when he sees, hears or smells something new.

In this chapter, I detail my gentle, confidence-building sack-out technique. Start by holding an item away from your horse, gradually working closer to him as he relaxes. Then gently rub his entire body, starting with his shoulders and gradually working to the head and down the hind legs. When he's completely relaxed with you rubbing him all over, progress to other items.

To do this lesson safely, your horse must willingly stand tied, and not have a history of signaling threats. (See "Behavioral Issues" below.)

Simple Solution

1. Tie your horse. Outfit your horse in a rope halter and lead. Tie him to a sturdy, stable post in your round pen, or to the panel only if it's secured to a post, so he doesn't get hurt if he spooks or pulls back. Tie him on a short rope, at or above withers level, to avoid having him get a foot caught or you tripping over the rope. Use a quick-release knot so you can quickly undo the rope in an emergency. Carry a foldable or sheathed knife in case the knot does not release and your horse needs assistance.

Recognize that a tantrum is not an emergency. Releasing your horse when he throws a tantrum is doing him a lifetime of disservice. Instead, allow him to feel the pressure as long as he's not in danger. This is the best way for him to learn that it's much easier to stand tied than fight the pressure.

2. Start at a distance. Hold your first object at a distance from your horse, as shown, allowing him to look at it. When he relaxes, slowly wave the object, accustoming him to the movement and sound. If he tenses, back away, slow your movement and even stop to encourage him to settle down. Then slowly begin again, and gradually work up to waving the object. Once your horse accepts the waving object, slowly move around him, from one side to the other, until he relaxes. Work closer to him, continuing to show him the object, allowing him to inspect it, and then waving it. Return to his previous comfort zone any time he becomes nervous.

3

Work from the shoulders up the neck. Start by rubbing the object gently against your horse's shoulder, as shown. As he relaxes, work up the side of his neck. Return to the shoulder if he tenses, then slowly work up the neck again. As he accepts having his neck rubbed, rub down his shoulder to reinforce his relaxation.

4. Move to the front leg. When your horse accepts rubbing on his neck, slide the object down his front leg to his foot. Remain beside your horse, staying close to his body and facing his hindquarters, to avoid being kicked. Keep your free hand on his neck to sense any reaction and to brace yourself. Should he become tense or frightened, rub back to the shoulder until he relaxes, then slowly progress back down the leg. Repeat until he accepts rubbing down his leg without incident.

5. Progress to the back, hips and hind legs. Slowly work along your horse's back, hips and down his hind legs while resting your free hand on him. Move slowly, especially if your horse shows signs of nervousness. As before, return to his previous comfort zone if he tenses.

Once you've sacked out one side of your horse, introduce other objects, one at a time, in the same manner. Here, I've switched sides. It's important to work around your horse so he's confident with you working on both sides of his body.

6 **Rub his head.** When your horse has accepted the object on the rest of his body, slowly wor the object toward his head. If your horse spooks or jerks his head aside, rub the object dow his neck and shoulder to build his confidence. Then work back to his face so you don encourage spooky behavior. If he's nervous, work back down his neck until he relaxes, the slowly work up his neck toward his head again. Work up around his ears in the same gradu manner. As he accepts the sensation, work to rub his forehead. Each time he tenses, mov back down his neck until he relaxes, then back to his head for a longer duration, until he comfortable.

When your horse is comfortable with an array of objects touching him, get ready to h the trail and continue your spook-control training with the exercise outlined in Chapte 8: "Ride Through the Fear."

Sacking out your horse with a saddle blanket is the first step toward smooth saddling.

Behavioral Issues

This simple sack-out procedure is effective on horses that understand the proper relationship with humans. It's not appropriate for horses with disciplinary issues, either vicious or what we call "spoiled" horses. A horse that resents correction or discipline, retaliates against the handler without hesitation, or does everything at his own pace must be handled with additional caution.

A horse that enjoys your rubbing, brushing and treats can still fit into the category of spoiled. Horses that fit my definition of "spoiled" don't come from abusive homes, but rather from loving homes with inadequate discipline. It's extremely important that horse owners or trainers diagnose and recognize this problem. Such horses are dangerous to themselves and their owners. When the spoiled horse must mentally deal with not having control, such as being tied adequately, or getting hung up in the trailer, brush or vines, the reaction is often violent, which surprises the owner or rider. The

NECESSARY EQUIPMENT

- **Halter and lead rope.** I use a hand-tied rope halter with a 10-foot lead. I prefer this type of halter to the typical leather or nylon web halter because it offers me more control and helps gain my horse's attention. Horses, like people, generally take the path of least resistance. A rope halter makes it comfortable for the horse to stand and accept the training, and uncomfortable if he attempts to pull away.

  This type of halter is also easier to inspect for weakness, and it's easier to cut off in an emergency. (The latter shouldn't be an issue if you've done your homework.)

- **Round pen.** For safety, I prefer a 60-foot round pen with soft ground and 6-foot-high, durable horse-safe panels. Five-foot-tall panels invite horses to try to jump, and generally they get on the panels, crush them and are out. Make sure your pen is free of sharp edges or hazards that could cause injury. Cattle panels typically

have flat metal reinforcement members that can take out a chunk of a knee or ankle.

- **Barn and household items.** Pick items of various sizes, shapes, textures, sounds, etc. Items to consider include: a plastic poncho, rain parka or plastic tarp, your child's musical instruments, metal can or bucket filled with marbles or marble-sized gravel, a leaf blower, the neighbor's skid loader or a tractor with a front-end loader, a barn cat (the cat at my barn jumps on schooling mares' backs without invitation), a swinging whip and a rope. Use a little imagination and much common sense. The number of items you should use on your horse depends on his disposition and training level. If you have a green youngster or a skittish horse, you might need to sack him out with several items to encourage him to resist his urge to flee. On the other hand, a quiet, willing horse might require sacking out with only a few items.

reaction might not come for several minutes. Previously unseen bucking or rearing and crashing over backwards are common reactions. If you even suspect this may be an issue, wait to begin your training until you can seek professional help from a horseman who commonly deals with behavioral issues. Generally 15 minutes in a round pen is enough time for an experienced trainer to diagnose a spoiled horse.

KINSEY'S KEYS TO SUCCESS

- **Watch your horse's body language.** This can be tricky, but it's critical. Handle instinctual reactions with understanding and tenacity. Behavioral issues require discipline. If you don't recognize the difference, seek help from a knowledgeable horse person. If you handle the situation incorrectly, you might send the wrong signals to your horse and teach him bad habits or to fear you—the opposite of your objective. (See "Behavioral Issues" for more.)

  As a rule, if the training gets exciting, from your perspective, not the horse's, you might be pushing your horse too hard, and you might be out of control. You want to work at the edge of the horse's comfort zone. Watch for signs of nervousness, alarm or fear, moving slowly or just backing off until he relaxes, then try again. Common signs of nervousness are staring, raising his head and pricking his ears forward at the object. If you get to the point that the horse is leaning back with his front feet extended, snorting, pulling back on the halter or swinging his head, looking for a place to run, and sweating and trembling in extreme cases, you're pushing too much.

  In these situations, patience and persistence are the key. Return to rubbing an object or area in his comfort zone. Then slowly try again as he's ready.

- **Allow plenty of time.** Take whatever time necessary to accustom your horse to an object, progressing only when he's comfortable. He'll lower his head, relax and not pay attention to the object when he's calm. I generally spend 15 minutes of intensive training per session for each year of age, with a maximum of 45 to 60 minutes. For example, I'd spend 15 minutes per session for a yearling. Sometimes I might perform two or three sessions on the same horse in a day. Your goal is to work for success, not time.

- **Work slowly.** Quick movements could startle your horse, defeating the purpose of this exercise. Our objective is to familiarize and build confidence, not to scare the horse, so start, for example, with your blanket initially folded up, then with each pass unfold it a bit more.

- **Work both sides.** Rub each object on both sides of your horse. Just because your horse accepts an object on one side doesn't mean he'll tolerate it on the other side, and you want to be able to work on both sides.

- **Stay out of kicking range.** When working around your horse's hind legs, keep your head away from his feet and avoid standing behind him, where you could get kicked. Instead, remain at his side, walking several feet behind him when changing sides. Avoid getting cow-kicked. Approach and work initially at, and from, the horse's shoulder. If kicking or biting is an issue, recognize you may have a behavioral problem stemming from learned disrespect. The remedy is discipline, not just training. You may need to consider getting professional help.

- **Watch the head.** Head blows are more common than kicks. If your horse pulls back, rearing or whipping his head side to side, get out of the way to avoid a head injury. After a horse pulls back, he often lunges forward, sometimes with his front feet up and out where they could strike you, or he might head-butt you. If you experience this type reaction, you've passed completely through the horse's comfort zone, or you're seeing a tantrum.

- **Tie him like you mean it.** Pulling back can be a good lesson for a horse. But if the horse pulls back, jerking the rope loose and getting away, that's undesirable. If I can't get a knot loose, I can cut it. I can afford to buy a new lead rope or halter easier than I can afford a lifetime of repetitive training to correct the bad habits a horse learns when the equipment breaks and he gets away.

  To avoid this, tie your horse securely to a sturdy post, buried several feet in concrete in the ground. A weak post, or one buried 2 feet in the ground, even with concrete, is a recipe for danger and disaster. If a horse pulls back, I want him to learn that if he gives the slightest bit, the pressure immediately releases. Don't use inner tubes or bungee cords as alternatives, as these gimmicks often break and your horse is required to give several inches to get a release reward.

- **Keep your horse's best interest in mind.** Make decisions that positively affect your horse and his long-term training. Too often folks make decisions based on what makes the person feel good about the training, not what's in the best interest of the horse. This often requires tough love.

Teach your trail horse the foundation of forward motion, and improve his response to rein cues, with this ground-driving method.

7

GROUND-DRIVING

I start every horse I work using this ground-driving technique because it provides fundamental control skills, such as moving forward, turning, stopping and backing. Furthermore, ground-driving accustoms your horse to flapping objects around his legs and to you working behind him. You can be insistent that your horse complies with your cues without the risk of him hurting you or resisting to the point of creating a training problem.

Ground-driving also allows you to assess a horse's skills and attitude, and increases his confidence and control from the ground, so he'll be safe and secure when you ride him. Ground-driving benefits an older horse that's balky, stiff on one side or simply lacks the basics. Once your horse is comfortable ground-

NECESSARY EQUIPMENT

- **35-foot driving lines.** I buy 100-foot lengths of $3/8$-inch diameter, braided nylon rope, cut two 35-foot sections and secure snaps to the ends. Avoid a solid line with snaps on each end. If your horse takes off, the line might catch behind your knees, making you a human plow. Cotton lines are heavy when damp, and leather lines are slippery when wet, as well as expensive. I have tried some of the synthetics, such as beta, which looks and feels like leather, with success.

- **Bridle with a smooth-mouthed snaffle bit and chin strap.** This bit gives you direct contact with your horse's mouth. Secure a chin strap, or bit hobble, to the rings to prevent pulling the bit through your horse's mouth.

- **Round pen.** For safety, I prefer a 60-foot round pen with soft ground and 6-foot-high, durable, horse-safe panels. The area also should be free of sharp edges or obstacles that could injure your horse or catch your lines.

- **Saddle and blanket.** Go ahead and saddle your horse as though you were going to ride him.

- **Durable rope, rein or strap.** Use this to tie your stirrups together.

- **Pair of gloves.** Unless your hands are pretty tough like mine, gloves are a good idea to prevent burns if a line slides through your hand.

driving, the principles apply when you step into the saddle.

Here, I show you my ground-driving method to help you start your trail mount right. For maximum results, begin driving an old, reliable horse so you can get the hang of handling the lines. Your horse should have the following skills before you continue:

- Lead and back in response to lead-rope pressure from the ground.

- Willingly perform basic round-pen work under saddle.

- Move away from you in response to a "kiss" cue.

- Drag a pair of ropes without fear.

- Accept the snaffle bit and being "bitted-up," when you tie a rein to the rear girth's D-ring so the horse's head is pulled 15 to 30

degrees to one side or the other, so he yields laterally to rein pressure. He also should be accustomed to being bitted up with light contact from both reins just enough that he's not frightened when restrained.

- Accept hobbles.

Preparation

If you take shortcuts, you might be in for a frustrating experience. Follow these steps to ensure your horse will be prepped for successful ground-driving.

Saddle and bridle your horse, and enter your round pen. I prefer to start ground-driving in a round pen. It's easy to transition from warming up a horse to driving him in an environment in which he's comfortable. Also, in a round pen he can't escape and hurt himself should he panic and you lose the lines. Plus, there are no corners for him to charge into, reducing the risk of him jumping the fence or breaking through it.

Use the following tips to assemble your driving outfit:

1. Using a sturdy strap or rein, securely tie your stirrups together underneath the horse's belly so they won't flap. Tie high on each stirrup and around the stirrup hobble (the leather that wraps around the top of your stirrup) for maximum stability. Make sure that the stirrups are below your horse's belly, so you don't inadvertently pull up his head with the driving lines.

2. Attach a driving line to each snaffle ring, behind the chin strap. If you use scissor snaps, place the triggers on the outside so they don't rub your horse's cheeks.

3. Starting on the right side, run the driving line from the snaffle through the stirrup on the same side. Hang the coiled driving line from your saddle horn. Then change sides, and run the left driving line from the left snaffle ring through the same-side stirrup. Hold the line in your left hand, at an angle to your horse's body.

4. Slowly pick up the right line with your right hand and run it behind your cantle. The left driving line should be on your left side, and the right line should be on your right side, but

both line ends should be together on the same side of the horse. That helps prevent tangles and allows you to quickly grab the lines if your horse suddenly moves.

Procedure

1. Get into safe position. Have your helper hold your horse while you gather your lines and establish proper position. Stand about 20 feet behind and about 45 degrees to the side of your horse, and hold a line in each hand. Positioning yourself at 45 degrees allows you to be close enough to minimize the amount of rein drag and shorten the distance you walk as compared to the distance your horse travels. The shorter travel distance means that you can keep up even if your horse begins to run. This position also keeps you out of the kicking and/or blind spot directly behind the horse, enhancing safety and reducing your horse's stress and uneasiness.

Close your fingers firmly around the driving lines and keep your thumbs up. Don't grip your lines too tightly or you might inadvertently apply too much bit pressure. Also, avoid wrapping the lines around your hands; if your horse takes off, your hands could get caught and you can be dragged. Allow the excess line to drag behind you, so you can quickly lengthen or shorten the lines as necessary.

2. Go forward. Initially, your primary goal is to get your horse to move, whether it is at a walk, trot or run. At this point, it's important that you avoid overcontrolling your horse until he learns to move forward. If you confuse or frustrate him early on, it takes longer for him progress to the next step.

Once you're in position, have your helper release your horse and move to the side, rather than in front of the horse. So your helper doesn't get caught in your lines, make sure you guide your horse straight or slightly

to the right, using right-line pressure, as your helper backs away and moves behind you.

Kiss to your horse to encourage him to move forward. Once he starts to move, things can happen fast and furiously, so be prepared for anything. Follow at a safe distance, keeping enough slack in your lines to avoid constant contact and sending him a stop signal. Raise your hands high enough to prevent the lines from dragging the ground. When you start, don't deter forward movement. Let your horse circle the pen a few times before you begin to gradually establish control and communicate through the lines.

Problem-Solving Strategies
- If your horse doesn't move, bump his hips with the lines, as shown in Photo 2. If that doesn't work, you haven't properly prepared him for this maneuver. Practice

the basic round-pen work outlined in Chapter 4 until he responds to your voice commands.

- If your horse gets out of control, or you feel as though either of you is in danger, turn him into the rail, using the cues outlined in Step 3, and then drive him in the opposite direction just as you would use defensive riding techniques. You might need to change direction several times to gain control. Once he's settled down and you're in control, drive him until he quietly walks or trots. In worst-case scenarios, you can drop the lines. In the round pen, your horse can't go very far.

- If your horse steps over a line with a hind leg, continue to drive him forward. You can still control him with a line between his legs. However, don't allow the line to wrap

3

around a leg. If this happens, stop your horse using the cues outlined in Step 5. Have your helper hold your horse while you regroup and start again.

3. Circle and turn. When your horse willingly walks along the rail, begin walking circles and using direct-line pressure to guide him. To work your horse on a left-hand circle, as shown in Photo 3, step toward the inside of the circle, so you don't have to travel as far as the horse to keep up. Smoothly lift your direct (left) line and remove the slack. Then apply gentle pull-and-release pressure on that line to encourage him to tip his nose toward the inside of the circle. Keep your indirect (right) line loose to avoid confusion. When your horse tips his nose in the direction of the turn, even if it's only slightly, release your pressure as a reward and to allow him

to turn freely. With repetition, your horse learns that if he yields to the pressure, he gets relief. Then he starts flexing his neck on cue. Use the opposite cues when driving your horse to the right.

When you get the desired response consistently, you're ready to change direction. I prefer to initially turn toward the fence for safety. I don't want the horse moving away from me too fast during the turns.

4. Switch direction. To move from a left-hand circle with you on the left to a right circle with you on the right, release your line pressure and build a safe distance behind your horse. While cueing him to turn with the right line, allow the left line to feed through your hand while he moves forward. Increasing your right-line pressure tips his head to the right. As he begins the transition you should

be moving from his left hip to his right one, keeping a safe distance. Use give-and-take pressure to guide him through the turn.

Kiss and use body language to encourage your horse to walk out of the turn. My body language includes raising my hands, lifting my chin and stepping a bit closer to him with authority. Next, step to the inside of the circle, shortening the right line and continuing to lengthen your left line while guiding your horse on a circle. Reverse these cues for a right-to-left turn. Practice direction changes until you and your horse perform them smoothly.

Problem-Solving Strategies

• If your horse is overflexed, and resists moving into a smooth circle, resulting in both his rear and his head pointing into the circle, apply light outside-line pressure as necessary to keep him aligned with the arc of the circle, and drive him forward to follow his nose.

• If your horse resists the pressure, increase your line pressure to tip his nose to the inside of the circle and bump his outside hip with the outside line to push him into a circle. If he continues to resist force-

fully, he hasn't been schooled well during your bitting sessions. Go back and review, leaving him bitted up on each side for 30 to 45 minutes for several lessons, if necessary. Don't bit him and pull his head past 30 degrees. Generally, that causes him to develop a "rubber neck," overflexing while continuing to walk forward.

5. Stop. I use a simultaneous two-cue process, with an immediate follow-up if needed. To stop your horse, apply light, equal tension on both lines, making contact with his mouth, as in Photo 5. Simultaneously say "whoa"

to reinforce your line cues. The instant he stops, cease your pressure to reward him with release and verbal praise. Wait 15 or 20 seconds before asking your horse to move again. With practice he learns to stop in response to light contact and, better yet, simply your voice command.

Problem-Solving Strategies

- If your horse doesn't stop, or steps through the stop, as if coasting through a stop sign, support your whoa cues by turning him into the rail and alternating line pressure to encourage him to stand and face the rail.

This barrier prevents him from moving forward. (On the trail I use bushes and big trees as barriers.) Establish early on that the pressure and voice cues mean for him to stop and stand.

- When driving in an open area, where you might not have a physical barrier, use a different stop sequence. As with stopping in a round pen, apply gentle line pressure and say, "whoa." This time, however, also brace your body against the lines, forming a barrier.

6. Back. Backing further develops your control, thus increasing your safety. Start by walking your horse briskly, then quickly turn him into the rail and signal him to stop. Next, pause for a half-second, releasing the lines. Then say "back" just before you apply firm, give-and-take backward pressure on the lines, as in Photo 6. Your horse already is collected, with his hind legs reaching under his belly, so he should naturally step backward for balance. Reward any effort by releasing the line pressure, followed by an extended pause and verbal praise. Repeat this step, gradually asking him to take one more step at a time and developing his responsiveness to light contact, until he backs freely. With repetition, your horse figures out that he's supposed to step backward when he feels the light pressure. Once your horse consistently stops and backs five or six steps, you're ready to hit the trail.

Problem-Solving Strategies
- At first your horse might back crooked. Use your driving lines to help straighten him. For example, if he backs to the left, step to the right just enough that you're off center, and apply a bit more left-line pressure to straighten his body. This aligns his head to back in the correct direction, and the extra pressure on his hip reminds him to move away from the pressure into the correct position.

- If your horse doesn't respond to your back-up cues, alternate line pressure. If he still doesn't respond, you might not have communicated your point clearly in your initial lessons. Return to the previous step until your horse is ready. Forcing your horse to back only results in a fight that hinders future training efforts.

KINSEY'S KEYS TO SUCCESS

- **Train yourself first.** Practice with a calm, seasoned horse that's comfortable ground-driving until you're confident in your ground-driving skills. Focus on feeling your horse through the lines and adjusting line length without looking at your hands.

- **Seek support.** If you're not comfortable ground-driving your horse, seek help from a knowledgeable horseman.

- **Start in a round pen.** Only when your horse is reliably responsive to your cues and you're confident in your control should you work in a larger area, such as an arena or pasture, or on the trail.

- **Mentally condition your horse.** Before you ground-drive your horse, work him in a round pen or longe him to take off the edge, focus his attention on you and put him in a learning mindset. I know a horse is ready to work when he turns toward me and follows me.

- **Train for success.** You have four objectives in this lesson: go, turn, stop and back. Don't progress to the next objective until your horse clearly understands the previous one. This could take any amount of time, depending on his training and willingness. Advancing too quickly causes confusion and frustration for both of you. Instead, take as much time and as many repetitions as necessary, and reward the smallest success.

- **Take it slow.** Work your horse in 10- to 20-minute increments, especially if he's a youngster, to prevent boredom.

- **Use precise cues.** When you consistently cue your horse, you avoid confusion, thus speed up his progress.

- **Monitor line length.** Don't let the lines drag the ground or pull on your horse's mouth; otherwise, you increase the risk of you or your horse getting tangled, and you send mixed messages.

- **Stand back and slightly to the side.** The closer you can be to your horse, and remain safe, the more quickly and effectively you can cue him. Initially, stand about 20 feet behind and slightly to one side of your horse, so you're out of kicking range, and he can clearly see you. As he starts moving, reduce the distance to about 10 feet.

- **Moving is a priority; control is your objective.** At first, your horse might take off and run laps in the round pen. Move with him until he slows down. Turn him into the rail and send him the opposite way to help slow him down and gain control. Once he figures out there's nothing to fear, he'll settle down.

8

RIDE THROUGH THE FEAR

Y ou're on a trail ride, pointing out scenery and wildlife to your riding buddy, when suddenly your horse jumps to the side, dodging the horse-eating monster lurking in the bushes. His heart pounds, and he freezes in his tracks, raises his head and focuses on the spooky object, which turns out to be a blowing branch. Shaky in the saddle, you wonder if the rest of your ride will be this nerve-wracking.

If your horse is terrified of things along the trail, you must build his confidence and trust in you, and you must become an alert, active rider, anticipating scary stimuli and gaining control before he can take charge. Otherwise he or you could get hurt.

83

My horse is arching his neck and pointing his ears forward, and he's starting to lean as though he's about to jump sideways and spook from the bridge railing.

A raised head, wild eyes and tense muscles are other signs that your horse is afraid and might spook.

Here, I explain why your horse reacts so skittishly to foreign sights, sounds and smells and show you how to ride through his fear.

Before you begin, sack out your horse using the steps outlined in Chapter 6. This accustoms him to various objects being waved around and touching his body. Plus, it helps develop his confidence so he doesn't turn tail and run at every strange sensation. He also should have the following skills:

• Move forward, backward and stop readily.

• Yield laterally to direct-rein pressure in both directions.

Spook Clues

Horses evolved as prey animals and have a natural herd instinct for survival. Spooky behavior stems from the same instinct. Spooking, also known as flight-or-fight behavior, is a horse's natural survival mode. Your horse has evolved to use all his senses to constantly check for strange sights, smells or sounds that might indicate a predator and, thus, the need to run for his life.

Just because your horse is wired to spook doesn't mean you have to tolerate his terrified behavior. Sure, you must acknowledge his natural flight-or-fight instinct. However, if you learn to recognize spook clues in your environment and his body language, you can be ready to handle the problem. For example, your horse might be more apt to spook when he hasn't been worked and is feeling playful, or during windy or stormy weather or in an unfamiliar environment.

Signs of spooking include becoming excited, tensing his muscles, raising his head, pointing his ears forward and/or snorting. But you can reduce the severity of his spook and, in some cases, teach him to "spook in place" by developing his confidence, sharpening your communication and diverting his attention from the scary stimuli and to your guidance and control.

Simple Solution

1. Read his body language. As you ride, look ahead for possible spooky spots, and monitor the horse for signs of spooking. If you think your horse might spook, place one hand on each rein and be ready to take charge of the situation with direct-rein control. Your goal: Anticipate his urge to flee, and keep him

NECESSARY EQUIPMENT

- **Bridle with a smooth-mouthed snaffle bit, chin strap (bit hobble) and split reins.** Split reins and a snaffle give you direct-rein control, while a properly adjusted chin strap prevents pulling the bit through your horse's mouth. Keep in mind: A snaffle is distinguished by its lack of shanks, while a curb has shanks for leverage. Some riders refer to a Tom Thumb or Argentine snaffle as a snaffle, because it has a broken mouthpiece, but its shanks make it a curb. (See the American Quarter Horse Association 2008 Official Handbook of Rules & Regulations, rule #443 [b] and [c].) If you pull on a rein attached to a shank, you don't have the direct-rein contact you have with a snaffle.

- **Saddle and blanket (or pad).**

moving under control. You might not be able to move him toward the object, but you can make him move in the direction you specify.

2. Turn toward the object. If your horse spooks, or acts as though he might, perform a training maneuver, such as circling or riding a serpentine, to focus his attention on you. Ride two-handed for direct contact with his mouth. If you allow him to stop and fixate on the object, you lose his attention—and your control. If your horse spooks and attempts to turn and run, calmly, confidently and immediately use direct-rein pressure to turn him toward the scary stimuli, and then perform a training maneuver. This prevents him from developing the habit of bolting away from scary objects. Bolting is much more dangerous than jumping sideways. The worst that can happen with the sideways spook is that you get slightly bruised physically and mentally. On the other hand, a horse that bolts acts irrationally, putting himself and his rider at risk for running into traffic, off embankments, into fences and other dangerous situations.

Problem-Solving Strategies

- Resist the urge to pull back on the reins when your horse spooks—a common reaction I notice in novice riders. If you pull back on the reins, you risk teaching your horse he's stronger than you, creating a potential runaway situation. Plus, your horse might throw his head and rear. To avoid a fight you can't win, it's best to use smooth, consistent direct-rein cues to turn him where the two of you can remain safe.

- If your horse braces against the rein pressure and refuses to turn, increase the intensity of your cues, tipping his nose in the direction you want to go. Drive him forward firmly with your seat and legs.

- Recognize that spooking in place isn't always negative behavior. In extremely spooky horses that might be an acceptable compromise.

- Avoid punishing your horse for spooking. Instilling the thought of pain or punishment when he's frightened only escalates the problem. To reduce his flight-or-fight instincts, you must consistently apply proper techniques to instill good habits.

3. Work in your horse's comfort zone. Once you turn your horse, immediately circle or weave 10 to 20 steps away from the spooky spot. I'm starting to circle my horse in this photo. Perform a familiar maneuver away from the area to allow him to enter his comfort zone, where he relaxes and listens to you. Remain calm and use consistent cues, assuring your horse there's nothing to fear.

Problem-Solving Strategies
- Monitor your horse's body language. If he doesn't relax, you haven't reached his comfort zone. Move him farther away from the obstacle until he stops worrying about it.

4. Encourage him to relax. Continue to work your horse in his comfort zone until he relaxes, complies with your cues and moves willingly. With both hands on the reins for direct-rein control, work toward the spook-producing spot, performing the same maneuver to keep his mind off the scary stimuli and locked on you. Return to your horse's comfort zone if he gets upset. Use direct-rein pressure to keep his nose pointed in the direction you want. Here, I'm asking my horse to serpentine, moving closer to the scary object in small increments until we're next to it. If it's possible, move around the feared object in this manner to further build his confidence.

Problem-Solving Strategies
- If, at any time, your horse gets nervous and shows signs of spooking, return to the previous spot in his comfort zone, repeating the maneuver. Then gradually work to expand his comfort area.

- As you move around the object, remember to circle in both directions, exposing both sides of your horse to the object.

5. Work toward the scary stimuli. When you reach the object, stop and allow your horse to rest near it. He might look at the object out of the corner of his eye, but use direct-rein pressure to prevent him from turning to look at it. Your goal is to convince him to trust your judgment—to accept your guidance over his fear. Allowing him to look at the object defeats that purpose. If you've done the exercise correctly, your horse should approach the object and stop without hesitation, because he's confident and attentive to you. Now you're ready to ride without

5

reservation, because you have a sure-fire way to settle your spooky horse.

Problem-Solving Strategies

- Make sure your horse's attention is focused on you, not the object. You know he's listening to you when he responds readily to your cues and flicks one or both ears toward you. If he points his ears toward an object or turns to look at it, return to the previous point and start again. You want him so comfortable that he doesn't pay attention to the object.

- If he "peeks" at the object, flicking an ear toward it, continue your training maneuver until he no longer notices the object. Then slowly move closer to it.

Roadside Safety

There's always a chance your horse might spook at a plastic bag, a neighbor's barking dog, a mailbox or any other object. But it's extremely dangerous if he spooks near a busy road, into the path of a vehicle doing 55 miles an hour. This is one of the worst scenarios I face with young or green horses and novice riders. Here are tips to handle this potentially fatal situation.

- **Use common sense.** To avoid the situation altogether, don't take green horses or novice riders near roads. Even while riding an experienced horse, be alert, anticipate what might scare your horse and be ready to take control with direct-rein pressure. Watch for drivers who honk or throw things from the car, or drivers who focus on the horse, allowing their vehicles to drift in the direction of their gaze. To keep you and your horse safe, you must pay attention and be ready for anything.

- **Ride two-handed.** Don't wait until your horse spooks to take charge. Ride with a hand on each rein so you're in constant control.

- **Keep the horse between your legs and reins—mentally and physically.** Rather than allow your horse to walk along the road and look around, be an active rider and train with every step, especially in situations where he might spook. If you anticipate a problem, move his nose an

Using direct-rein and leg pressure, keep your horse with you mentally and physically to prevent him from drifting into traffic.

My horse is shying from something scary in the distance on my right. I turn him toward the object to prevent him from scooting onto the road, where a car could hit him.

inch to the left with direct-rein pressure, asking him to flex. Then release and allow him to walk a couple of steps. Repeat or perform another maneuver. This keeps him focused on you, and he is less likely to notice the fear-inducing objects. Keep him busy, as with a child, to prevent him from getting in trouble, plus develop his skills. Furthermore, if he spooks, you already have his attention, so you can take control of the situation.

- **Take immediate action.** Be ready to immediately turn your horse toward the object of his fear with direct-rein pressure, moving him away from the road.

- **Use obstacles and distance.** If you notice something that could spook your horse, try to ride with the object between you and the road, so your horse shies away from traffic, rather than into the road. For example, keep a ditch between you and the road.

KINSEY'S KEYS TO SUCCESS

- **Begin in the round pen.** Before you ride your horse, work him on the longe line or in a round pen to expend some of his nervous energy and to get his focus.

- **Be an alert, active rider.** Learn to recognize "ambush areas"—places where your horse becomes naturally suspicious and nervous, such as a dark, narrow trail. Look ahead and anticipate spooky situations, so you can prepare and take charge.

- **Disregard his motivation.** Whether your horse is truly afraid, or just fresh and trying to test you, your actions should be the same: Perform a maneuver until he's either confident or not willing to play silly games. Unlike previous lessons, this is one time you shouldn't worry about instinct versus attitude, correction versus discipline. It's tough to tell the difference during spooking. If you treat it as an instinctual issue, you always win. If you treat it like a disciplinary problem, you could be wrong and scare your horse even more.

- **Forget force.** If you force your horse toward a scary object, you only create a fight you lose. Instead, be patient, building your horse's confidence and laying a lasting foundation of willingness and trust.

- **Take off the tie-down.** Some riders resort to tie-downs to keep their horse's heads down. In reality, most horses don't need tie-downs, and the additional stress can lead to rearing and fighting. Also, tie-downs can become a crutch for a rider's poor control techniques. Work for long-term cooperation, not a quick fix, gradually working through your horse's fear with consistent, proper training techniques.

Use these ground-driving and under-saddle techniques to school your horse over bridges and other trail obstacles.

9

CROSSING OBSTACLES

Backcountry trails are natural obstacle courses. At any moment you might be required to negotiate a log, bridge, ravine, water crossing or tough terrain, with no alternate route. However, such obstacles can frighten a horse (and rider) unfamiliar with them, and you definitely want to avoid a danger-ous situation on a steep, narrow trail. That's why it's important to accustom your horse to obstacles at home or on a familiar trail before you venture into new territory.

This and the next three chapters of this book focus on safely negotiating common trail obstacles. In this chapter, I explain how to introduce your horse to bridges. The method also applies to logs and ravines. In Chapters 10 and 11, I demonstrate how to safely negotiate brush and a water crossing, respectively; and finally, in Chapter 12, I cover negotiating tough terrain.

Recognize the difference between a horse that inspects an obstacle before crossing it and one that inspects it before deciding to cross. The latter might turn and bolt or kick.

To safely negotiate obstacles, your horse must have the following skills:

- Ground-drive willingly.

- Move forward, backward and stop readily.

- Yield laterally in both directions to direct-rein pressure.

- Confidently approach unfamiliar objects and obstacles.

Balking Basis

If you've been on enough trail rides, you know the scenario: As a horse approaches an obstacle, he points his ears forward and lowers his head to inspect the unfamiliar monster. Suddenly, he stops, snorts, and then panics and bolts. Or, he raises his head, pins his ears, swishes his tail in defiance, and refuses to heed the rider's direction and constant prodding.

Horses often balk at obstacles due to a combination of instinct, rider response and lack of discipline. As we've discussed in previous chapters, horses are programmed to

I place a tarp in my weanling and yearling pens so that young horses can check out and cross the obstacle on their terms. By the time they're ready to be ground-driven and even ridden, they're already accustomed to the tarp.

NECESSARY EQUIPMENT

- **35-foot driving lines.** I prefer two braided nylon rope lines, as opposed to a single line. If your horse bolts, the single line might catch behind your legs, and you'll be dragged.

- **Durable rope, rein or strap.** Use this to tie your stirrups together when ground-driving.

- **Pair of gloves.** Although I'm not wearing gloves in the photos, it's a good idea to prevent rope burns.

- **Bridle with a smooth-mouthed snaffle bit, chin strap (bit hobble) and split reins.** This headgear allows you to ride two-handed for direct-rein control. Secure a chin strap to the bit rings so you can fit only two fingers between the strap and your horse's chin. This prevents inadvertently pulling the bit through your horse's mouth.

- **Saddle blanket (or pad).** Avoid excessively thick pads that require so much cinch-tightening they cause equine discomfort or saddle slippage. Your horse's discomfort could distract him or cause him to resist your cues.

- **Riding partner with a reliable horse.** If your horse spooks or balks at obstacles, ask a riding buddy to cross the obstacle first. My assistants and I ride several young horses on the trail, but we always have a steady, seasoned mount in the group for the youngsters to emulate and follow.

- **Trail with low bridge, logs and gradual ravine.** For safety and to build your horse's confidence, start with small, low-to-the-ground obstacles, and gradually advance to more difficult ones. If you don't have access to a trail with these obstacles, and you don't have a bridge or logs at home, ask to borrow them from a local riding club.

anticipate predators. When they encounter something suspicious, their instinct is to fight or flee. Furthermore, they can't see close objects as well as faraway ones, so their perceptions of an obstacle might be inaccurate.

In other situations, rider tension creates the problem. Your anxiety radiates to your horse through your reins and legs, signaling him to become nervous. You might even inadvertently pull on the reins, telling him, "Don't go!" while tentatively trying to cue your horse forward.

Finally, some horses and riders simply lack control and communications. Whenever you allow a horse to balk and bolt from an obstacle, he learns that he can take control of the situation and do what he wants when he wants.

Before you begin to correct the problem, ask yourself whether your horse is truly fearful, or if he simply responds to what you signal him to do or what you allow him to do. Indeed, bridges, water and other obstacles look, sound and feel strange, but that doesn't mean you can't cross them. You simply must develop your and your horse's confidence and discipline so he relies on you to show him the way.

Groundwork Solutions

1. Ground-drive the horse. Introducing your horse to a bridge from the ground is a safe, surefire way to provide the foundation he needs to negotiate it under saddle. Plus, it reinforces your move-forward, stop and directional cues.

To reinforce your control and the correct response to ground-driving cues, first ground-drive your horse in the round pen, gradually progressing to an arena, then negotiating obstacles in the arena. Drive your horse across poles, as shown in Photo 1A, weave through poles or even cross a low bridge, as shown in Photo 1B.

To ground-drive your horse forward, kiss, bump his hips with the lines and use body language; step forward with authority and raise your hands. Follow about 15 to 20 feet behind and slightly to the side of your horse to avoid getting kicked. Also, hold your lines off the ground so your horse doesn't become tangled, and allow enough slack to avoid steady contact with his mouth.

On the trail, to obtain your horse's focus and establish forward motion, first drive him in an open area until he moves freely and responds readily to your cues. Then direct him toward the bridge. Remember that training is about setting up the situation for success. It's easier to cross an obstacle in the direction your horse wants to go, such as toward the barn, trailer or herd mates, than it is to cross in a direction he doesn't want to go. Therefore, plan your strategy, in or out of the arena, accordingly. For example, when on the trail, plan to cross the bridge on your way back to the trailer.

Problem-Solving Strategies
- If your horse is afraid to approach the bridge, drive him near it, as shown in Photo

If your horse slips off the bridge or is terrified to cross it, drive him forward beside the obstacle until he's confident.

1C, which is at the edge of his comfort zone. Then gradually move closer to the obstacle, as described in Chapter 8, "Ride Through the Fear." Continue to drive past the bridge until you sense the apprehension is gone.

- Don't settle for your horse's "I'll decide if I want to cross the obstacle" attitude. Instead, focus on ingraining your "let's go now" cues. Recognize the difference between a horse that inspects an obstacle before crossing it and one that inspects the obstacle before deciding to cross it. The latter might decide to turn and bolt or kick. He also might decide to buck with you in the saddle. Learning to recognize this behavior takes months of handling your horse. If your horse bullies you around the barn or round pen, or when you ride him, and you don't strongly reprimand him immediately, chances are he'll make the decisions at the obstacles, too.

- If your horse balks, but not due to a behavioral problem, follow a friend with a reliable horse across the bridge. Make sure the lead horse willingly crosses the obstacle. You don't want your horse to become frightened or unruly due to another horse's misbehavior. Allow the other horse to cross the bridge two or three times. If you or your horse is still nervous, follow closely behind the other horse several times until you're both confident.

- If your horse kicks, bucks or becomes surly when asked to approach the bridge, you have a disciplinary issue based on a lack of respect. This issue is much more far-reaching than just crossing obstacles. Resolve this dangerous issue with the help of a professional trainer before you attempt further training. Patience and repetition won't solve your horse's defiance; instead, you must confront the issue. Allowing your horse's threats to go undisplined encourages him to rebel whenever he's uncomfortable or unhappy, and you or your horse could be injured.

2. Keep your horse's nose pointed toward the bridge. Whether you're negotiating a bridge

on the trail or in the arena, as you approach and cross the obstacle, use direct-line pressure to keep your horse's nose pointed toward the bridge's entrance. This helps prevent the possibility of him turning or bolting away from scary objects.

If your horse attempts to turn away from the bridge, use the direct line to keep his nose aimed at the bridge. For example, if he turns left away from the bridge, apply right-line pressure, as shown in Photo 2A, to direct his face toward the obstacle. Keep your indirect (left) line loose to avoid sending mixed signals. Also, raise your hands and use body language to push him forward. When he tips his nose in the correct direction, release all pressure to reward him.

Approach the bridge briskly and confidently, allowing your horse, if he desires, to briefly inspect the obstacle. However, don't allow him to slow down for a rest or even think about balking; just drive him toward the obstacle.

At first, your horse might step gingerly onto the obstacle because the wooden surface and hollow sound are unfamiliar; that's okay as long as he moves forward. Praise your horse verbally for each step he takes, but keep him moving.

When your horse clears the bridge, praise him verbally and allow him to walk for a few seconds to savor his success. Then continue to build his confidence by driving a large circle and performing familiar maneuvers.

Problem-Solving Strategies
- If your horse is still afraid, cross the obstacle several times, until he relaxes. If you lead an out-of-control horse, he could injure you.

- If you feel your horse slow, waver or look around for alternate routes, gently yet firmly push him toward the obstacle with your voice and body language, while directing his nose in the direction you want to go, as in Photo 2B. To not only get your horse to cross the bridge, but to cross it with enthusiasm, intensify your cues and spank his hip with the lines if necessary.

- If your horse runs or jigs backward from the obstacle, don't tense and pull on the reins. Instead, relax, make your horse face the bridge and keep him moving. As long as your horse moves at your request, even if it's backward or sideways, you're on the right track.

- Your horse might walk halfway across the bridge and speed up or bolt the balance of the obstacle. If he takes off, don't over-react. Remain calm when he's past the point of return, and circle to slow him down. Then drive him away from the obstacle until he relaxes.

- Avoid becoming frightened and pulling back on the lines or your cues confuse your horse. Your goal is to encourage your horse forward and to negotiate the obstacle with confidence.

- Remain alert, anticipating your horse's every move. If he tenses and appears as though he might bolt, keep your elbows by your sides and be prepared to increase contact with his mouth, after he commits to crossing. If he bolts, he'll hit the bit barrier you've created.

- Mentally prepare for the unexpected. If your horse slips, slides or falls off the obstacle, continue to drive him forward through

and out of the obstacle area into a circle. Then try again. If you don't make a big deal of the obstacle, your horse learns that he need not either.

3. Repeat. Complete the circle at the bridge entrance. Then repeat this entire process several times until your horse is completely confident with negotiating the obstacle. In Photo 3, my horse is relaxed with level head carriage. This is the image of willingness and responsiveness you're trying to achieve.

Problem-Solving Strategies

- When praising your horse during training sessions, avoid the urge to hug or pet him. Otherwise, you risk tangling the driving lines in thick grass and brush, which crumbles the confidence you've worked so hard to build. Instead, use verbal praise and rest and pressure-release rewards.

Under-Saddle Solutions

1. Reinforce your cues. Just as you did in the ground-driving phase, begin riding in the round pen, gradually advancing to negotiating obstacles in an arena and open area as you develop control and your horse's responsiveness. If you have been consistent and firm with your "let's go now" cues from the ground, you should achieve the same response in the saddle. Accept no hesitation, reinforcing your cues as needed with leg cues or a rein swat. Don't negotiate a bridge in an open area until you have an immediate and controlled response in place.

Problem-Solving Strategies

- **Don't overdo it.** If your horse has a history of hesitating to move forward, take the time necessary to achieve improvement. Your goal is to reward your horse with stopping before he gets tired and quits. Before you get to the obstacle, your horse must understand that there's only one acceptable option to the "let's go now" cue. Any hesitation increases your chance for failure, and any failure at the crossing haunts your horse's training program.

2. Direct him across the bridge. When you're ready to cross the bridge, keep your horse's nose pointed directly at the obstacle entrance. Firmly and confidently encourage him across with leg pressure and voice cues. Reward his

2A

effort by staying out of his mouth. Initially, crossing a bridge with low rails, as shown in Photo 2A, might be less intimidating to your horse than crossing a bridge with high railings, as shown in Photo 2B.

As in the ground-driving exercise, your horse might move cautiously at first because his environment appears different with you on his back. Simply encourage him forward.

Don't check your horse by gently squeezing or pulling backward on the reins to prevent him from dashing across the obstacle. Once he's committed and can't back out, take control, but make sure you don't apply too much pressure or act too early, sending him mixed messages.

Repeat this step several times for several days to continue building your horse's confidence. Return home or to the trailer to reward his effort. When your horse is crossing consistently, dispense with riding directly home to unsaddle. If you're close enough to walk home or to the trailer, dismount, loosen the front cinch and lead him.

Problem-Solving Strategies
- Remember: If there's a direction in which your horse is comfortable crossing, for example, toward the barn or trailer, or on the way home from a trail ride, use that to your advantage.

KINSEY'S KEYS TO SUCCESS

- **Warm up your horse.** Before you attempt any training exercise, first warm up your horse in the round pen or on a longe line. Doing so burns his excess "playful" energy, increasing his learning capacity.

- **Train for control.** To develop your horse's control and confidence, take the time necessary to train in simple steps. Shortcuts often lead to danger and frustration, and usually require retraining.

- **Stay calm.** If you lose your temper or become nervous, your anxiety transfers to your horse and he's likely to become disobedient.

- **Cue consistently.** To ingrain the right response, cue your horse consistently, use an appropriate consequence and reward him regularly.

- **Call the shots.** First train your horse to approach the obstacle using the techniques outlined in Chapter

8. Then train him to cross the obstacle with the instructions presented in this chapter. The latter phase requires your horse to accept your control and guidance and that you're in charge and won't permit him to turn away. If your horse takes over, that mars past and future training.

- **Ask first, then correct.** Firmly cue your horse to cross the bridge. If he responds, release as a reward. If he doesn't respond, initiate the corrections outlined in this chapter.

- **Avoid whips and spurs.** If misused, these devices could frighten your horse—the opposite of your goal. Instead, persistently and consistently encourage your horse to do what you want, taking whatever time it takes to achieve success.

- **Seek support.** If you feel out of control or or in danger, it's best to stop and seek assistance from a professional trainer.

- Again, ask a riding buddy with a reliable horse to ride across the obstacle first so your horse can see there's nothing to fear.

- If you or your horse is particularly nervous, allow the horse to cross the first few times with his nose literally in the other horse's tail, as long as the other horse isn't prone to kick.

3. Expand his comfort zone. Once your horse is comfortable crossing the bridge, practice negotiating other obstacles, such as crossing logs and ravines, as shown in Photo 3. Use the same brisk "let's go now" strategies to get your horse across the first few times. Then build his comfort level and increase his control. In time, backcountry obstacles will become a walk in the park.

Prepare your horse for brush and branches so they don't become fear factors on the trail.

10

BRUSH AND BRANCHES

If you ride the backcountry, you encounter over- and under-brush, along with low branches, and there might not be another route. If your horse isn't accustomed to the pokes of brush and branches whapping and rubbing his body, they could make him spook, jump or bolt.

To help you prevent a panic situation out on the trail, I explain how to introduce your horse to bushes and branches in the safe confines of a round pen at home, applying concepts from the spook-control and sacking-out chapters. Then my assistant, Brianna Laston, shows how to safely navigate trail jungles.

Before you begin, your horse should have the following skills:

- Accept the sacking-out process.

- Move forward, backward and stop readily.

105

NECESSARY EQUIPMENT

- **Halter and lead rope.** I use a hand-tied rope halter with 10-foot lead. This type of halter provides more control and helps gain your horse's attention better than a nylon web or leather halter. It's also easy to inspect for weakness, and you can easily cut it off in an emergency.

- **Round pen.** For safety, I prefer a 60-foot round pen with soft ground or sand and 6-foot-high, durable horse-safe panels. Make sure your pen is free of sharp edges or hazards that could cause injury. A common mistake is saving a few bucks and buying 5-foot cattle panels. These typically have flat metal spacers that can cut knees and ankles. Occasionally, a playful or stressed horse jumps onto a 5-foot panel.

- **Tree-branch clipping.** Clip a full section with lots of leaves and branches that rustle.

- **Bridle with a smooth-mouthed snaffle bit and chin strap (bit hobble).** This bit allows you to ride two-handed and guide your horse in the direction you want. Secure a chin strap to the rings to prevent pulling the bit through your horse's mouth. Adjust the strap so you can fit only two fingers between the strap and your horse's chin.

- **Saddle and blanket (or pad).** To prevent slippage, secure a breast collar to your saddle and avoid using an overly thick pad.

- Yield laterally to direct-rein pressure in both directions.

Simple Solution

1. Turn your horse loose in a secure paddock or, preferably, the round pen. Place a small pile of branches and limbs in the round pen. From the ground, quietly but firmly work the horse around the pen until he does not become alert at the limbs.

2. Sack out your horse from a distance. Outfit your horse in a halter and lead, and tie him to a sturdy post in your round pen or to a panel only if it's attached to a sturdy post. Avoid tying him to cheap or light-duty corral panels. He could tear them apart and drag or fling them around if he pulls back—a dangerous situation for all involved. Tie him on a short rope, at withers level or higher, to avoid him catching a foot or you tripping over the rope. Tie a quick-release knot so you can quickly undo the line in an emergency.

Use the sack-out method outlined in Chapter 6 to introduce your horse to foliage touching his entire body. In the beginning, stand several feet to the side of your horse and gently wave the greenery to get him used

to the rustling and movement. Move into the edge of his comfort zone until he shows alarm, then quietly move away. Repeat this until he calmly allows you to stand next to him with the gently waving branches. Remember that by calmly retreating, you allow the horse time to assimilate that the branches don't harm him.

Problem-Solving Strategies
- If your horse tenses or pulls back, you're treading in uncomfortable territory. Slowly back away and hold the greenery still, allowing him to look at it, until he relaxes. Then slowly begin again, gradually waving the greenery more aggressively and working closer to your horse. Return to his comfort zone, the point he remains relaxed with the greenery, any time he becomes nervous.

- If your horse reacts violently to the greenery, and you feel as though you might be in danger, stop, allow him to settle and seek help from a professional horseman who deals with behavioral issues.

- Recognize that just because the horse pulls back and throws a tantrum doesn't mean you must try to untie him. Releasing a horse that is throwing a tantrum is guaranteed to produce more tantrums in the future.

- Do not tie the horse anywhere near a panel connection or anywhere he can get hung up should he pull back and lunge forward.

3. Allow your horse to inspect the greenery. Slowly approach your horse from the side with the greenery, where he can see you. I initially approach his left (near) side, the side he's accustomed to me working. Hold the greenery still and allow him to inspect it until it doesn't faze him. When he accepts the stimulus, he relaxes his head and neck, perhaps takes a deep breath and licks his lips.

Problem-Solving Strategies
- If your horse is tense like this horse, as indicated by his stiff stance, arched neck and forward ears, back away and perform Step 2 of this exercise to desensitize him to the scary stimuli.

4. Sack out his body. When your horse is comfortable with the waving greenery near his body, begin to sack out his entire body

with the branches. Standing at his shoulder, rather than in front of him, where he can't see you, gently and slowly stroke his shoulder with the tip of the twig. Then remove the stimulus and move away, allowing him to relax as a reward.

Next, rub his shoulder a little longer and more firmly. Repeat, removing the branches between repetitions for a reward, until your horse is comfortable with the greenery. Then use the same gradual technique to work up his neck, down his front leg, along his back and hips and down his hind leg. Repeat on the other side. Plan on using just as much time on the second side as you needed on the first.

Safety tip: When working around your horse's legs, position yourself to the side of and close to the leg you're working, and keep your head up, to avoid getting kicked. Move slowly and place your free hand on his body to anticipate any movement and to brace yourself.

Problem-Solving Strategies
- If your horse becomes nervous at any point, slow your motion and return to rubbing an area in his comfort zone.

5. Ride in the round pen. Once your horse accepts sacking out with the greenery, you're ready to try riding him around and through a pile of greenery in the round pen. Just as you worked the horse around other potentially scary items in the previous chapter, you now want to work the horse in and out of the edge of his comfort zone for the branches. Continue until the horse is relaxed riding near the brush, and then over the brush. Anytime the horse gets excited, turn him to keep him from running away from the scary item.

6. Plan a path. Once the horse is comfortable riding around and through your brush pile in the round pen, you're ready to ride in mild foliage on the trail. I start riding through an

overgrown pipeline or power-line right-of-way with 2- to 4-foot-high underbrush. This gives me ample room to turn around should the horse get excited. Plus, it keeps my head away from the limbs should my horse unexpectedly run. If a right-of-way isn't available, pick a relatively open trail with room to maneuver and minimal overbrush to set up your horse for success. Avoid heavy blackberry bushes or "wait-a-minute" vines during the initial rides, as these prickly plants are painful and irritating to a horse if he becomes entangled.

Ride two-handed for maximum control. Look ahead, watching for and anticipating obstacles. When you encounter a low-lying branch, look ahead to determine if you can direct your horse around the obstacle. That's always the best bet for safety. However, if you can't maneuver around the obstacle, ride confidently and firmly. Push through the brush without changing speed. If your horse spooks, quietly turn him around to disengage his hindquarters until he's quietly moving under control. Then continue down the trail.

Problem-Solving Strategies
- If your horse tenses, which he shouldn't when you've adequately prepared him for this work, resist the urge to pull back on the reins. Otherwise, you transmit apprehension to your horse and possibly confuse him. Plus, when you pull back, your horse braces against the pressure, and you are in a tug of war you can't win. Instead, use smooth, consistent direct-rein cues to turn your horse where you want him to go and send him forward with your seat and legs. (Refer to Chapter 8: "Ride Through the Fear," for tips on directing an apprehensive horse.)

- Don't allow your horse to stop. When your horse loses motion, you lose your ability to control his feet, creating frustration and a fight. If your horse tries to stop, use firm seat and leg pressure to keep him moving.

- Be calm and confident. If you transmit stress to the horse, he's likely to become stressed. Talking or singing often breaks the stress cycle.

7. Pass through the plants. Use direct-rein pressure to guide your horse in the direction you want—through the greenery. Drive him forward with a deep seat and leg pressure. Follow Step 6's problem-solving strategies to prepare him to smoothly pass through the greenery, as shown in the photo.

8. Repeat and reverse. When your horse quietly clears the greenery, reward him with rubs and a long moment of rest. Resting a minute or so when you stop your horse teaches him that stopping results in rest, not just a transition between movements. That little lesson

8

can pay big dividends if you get tangled in the vines and you want the horse to stand still while you get off and release him. After a moment of relaxation, turn around, if the trail permits, and pass through the obstacle from the other direction, to further his confidence. Use the same cues and problem-solving strategies outlined in Step 6. Repeat until your horse is completely confident to pass through mild brush and branches.

9. Go deeper into the forest. Gradually take your horse through thicker foliage, exposing him to over- and underbrush. When walking through thick willows or underbrush, allow your horse to slowly pick his way through the thicket, using your reins to guide him and your legs to keep him moving. Proper training results in your horse stoically traversing blackberry and prickly vines as just part of the job. If you encounter overhead branches, simply lean forward over your horse's neck to prevent getting hit by a wayward branch. Use the problem-solving strategies outlined in Step 6 to make the most of your trail training.

KINSEY'S KEYS TO SUCCESS

- **Watch your horse's body language.** This can be tricky, but it's critical for safely sacking out your horse. Handle instinctual reactions with understanding and tenacity and behavioral issues with discipline. If you don't recognize the difference, seek help from a knowledgeable horse person. Improper reactions might send the wrong signals to your horse and teach him bad habits or to fear you—the opposite of your objective. As a rule, if training gets out of hand, you might be pushing your horse too hard, and you're probably out of control. If your horse shows signs of nervousness, alarm or fear, move slowly and proceed carefully until he relaxes. Common signs of nervousness are staring, raising his head, pricking his ears forward at the greenery, leaning back with his front feet extended, snorting, pulling back on the halter or swinging his head, looking for a place to run, and sweating and trembling in extreme cases.

- **Work for success, not time.** Take whatever time necessary to accustom your horse to greenery, progressing only when he's comfortable. He lowers his head, relaxes and doesn't pay attention to the object when he's calm. This could take 15 minutes or several sessions.

- **Work slowly.** Quick movements could startle the horse, defeating the purpose of this exercise. Your objective is to familiarize and build confidence, not to scare him.

- **Watch his head.** Years of observations indicate that head-to-head blows are more common than kicks. If your horse pulls back, rearing or whipping his head side to side, get out of the way to avoid a head injury. After he pulls back, he might lunge forward, sometimes with his front feet up and out where they could strike you, or he might head-butt you.

- **Tie securely.** Pulling back can be a good lesson for a horse. But if he pulls back, jerks the rope loose and gets away, it's undesirable. To avoid this, tie your horse securely to a sturdy post, buried several feet into the ground with concrete. A weak post, or one buried shallowly in the ground, even with concrete, is a recipe for danger and disaster. If a horse pulls back, he should learn that a slight give on his part releases the pressure immediately. Don't use inner tubes or bungee cords as alternatives, as these gimmicks often break. Plus, your horse is required to give several inches to get a release reward.

- **Keep your horse's best interest in mind.** Make decisions that positively affect your horse and his long-term training. Too often folks make decisions based on what makes them feel good about the training, not what's in the horse's best interest. For example, some folks release a horse that's throwing a tantrum while tied. If you bail out the horse, you miss an opportunity to teach him that when he pulls back he causes discomfort to himself. Training often requires "tough love," but in the end you have a trusting, obedient mount.

Persuade your horse to negotiate water-crossings with these strategies.

11

TAKE THE PLUNGE

You're moseying down the trail when you approach a water-crossing. You tense and panic because your horse doesn't cross water. Last time he twirled, danced and reared along the water's edge, refusing to get his feet wet. Discouraged and frustrated, you cut your ride short or scouted a different route to settle him down. Now, sensing your anxiety, your horse becomes excited and begins to balk. "Here we go again," you tell yourself. "What should I do now?"

Become determined! You can avoid much frustration and danger on the trail, and explore more country by persuading your horse that he can cross water. Overcoming his hydrophobia begins at home, exposing him to water while doing groundwork. Then gradually introduce water to him under saddle. That's

115

what I outline in this lesson. First, however, I explain why horses fear water.

Before you attempt water-crossings, make sure your horse has the following foundation skills:

- Quietly stands tied.

- Ground-drives willingly.

- Moves forward, backward and stops readily on cue.

- Yields laterally to direct-rein pressure in both directions.

- Confidently approaches unfamiliar objects and obstacles.

What's the Big Deal with Water?

Your horse stands in the rain and drinks water every day, so why is it so spooky to step into it? First, ask yourself whether you contribute to his phobia by becoming nervous at water-crossings. Your apprehension, combined with the rein tugs that usually result from fear, signals your horse to become scared and stop.

Second, look back on past riding experiences. Have you allowed your horse to take control of the situation around scary stimuli or when he is uncomfortable, or when he does not want to cooperate? Do you allow him to buck, bolt and return to the barn or trailer when he becomes frightened or doesn't want to do what you ask? If you permit such tantrums, you must establish yourself as the leader and earn his trust and respect before you continue.

Finally, it also helps to understand the environment in which your horse is kept and his natural self-preservation instinct. If you're like many horse people, your horse is kept in a stall, paddock or pasture, where his only encounter with water is his water bucket. When he must cross water, is he allowed to do so at his own pace, at the spot he chooses

NECESSARY EQUIPMENT

- **Hose, spray nozzle and spigot.** Use these items to desensitize your horse to water on his legs. Buy a hose attachment that adjusts water pressure so you can gradually increase the pressure as your horse becomes comfortable.

- **Sturdy hitching post.** Tie your horse to spray his legs with the hose.

- **Halter and lead rope.** I prefer a rope halter with 10-foot lead for control.

- **35-foot driving lines.** I prefer two braided nylon rope lines, as opposed to a single line. If your horse bolts, the single line might catch behind your legs, and you'll be dragged. Though cotton lines are softer than nylon, they attract moisture and become heavy.

- **Round pen.** For safety, I prefer a 60-foot round pen with 6-foot-high, durable horse panels. The area also should be free of sharp edges or obstacles that could injure your horse or catch your driving lines. Using 5-foot-high panels is an invitation for a horse to attempt to jump the panels. Cattle panels commonly have intermediate supports that can gouge a knee or ankle.

- **Durable rope, rein or strap.** Use this to tie your stirrups together when ground-driving.

- **Pair of gloves.** Although I'm not wearing gloves, it's a good idea to prevent rope burns.

- **Bridle with a smooth-mouthed snaffle bit, chin strap (bit hobble) and split reins.** This headgear allows you to ride two-handed for direct-rein control. Secure a chin strap to the bit rings so you can fit only two fingers between the strap and your horse's mouth. Unbuckle this strap when bridling or removing the bridle.

- **Saddle and blanket (or pad).** Avoid overly thick pads that require excessive tightening and can cause equine discomfort and saddle slippage. Your horse's discomfort could distract him from the task at hand or cause him to resist your cues.

- **Experienced riding partner with a reliable horse.** If your horse spooks or balks at water, ask a riding buddy to cross the obstacle first. My assistants and I ride several young horses on the trail, but we rely on a steady, seasoned mount to show the youngsters the way the first couple of rides.

- **Trail with water-crossing.** For safety and to build your horse's confidence, start by first crossing a big puddle, and then later advance to a narrow creek and eventually a river.

My young horses spend time in a pasture with a pond. They learn to drink and cool off in the water, making it easier to get them to cross it on the trail.

and on his terms? Or does he perceive that the water-crossing is dangerous and must be handled with caution if he's not familiar with the water's depth or the footing? Furthermore, if you are inadvertently pulling on the reins while kicking and prodding, your confusing technique adds to the stress. Before long your horse associates punishment with water-crossings and becomes phobic.

Good news: In all these situations, you can overcome your horse's resistance to crossing water. The keys are time, patience, determination, consistency, clear guidance—and trust. Make the right thing easy for the horse and the wrong thing difficult, so before long your idea becomes his idea.

Groundwork Solution

Before you expose your horse to back-country water-crossings, acclimate him to water at home, using the following groundwork procedures. Working with your horse in a controlled, familiar environment reduces distractions so he can concentrate on you and the task at hand. Start slow and work in small, confidence-building steps your horse understands, and praise the slightest progress, so you build a strong foundation.

1. Spray water. Start by spraying water from a hose, the least intimidating option. Outfit your horse in a halter and lead and tie him to a solid post that can withstand the force should he pull back.

First introduce him to the sight and sound of water by turning the water on low and allowing it to flow from the hose, away from your horse. When the splashing water does not bother him, stand opposite his shoulder, about 6 to 10 feet away for safety, and gently mist his front feet.

When your horse relaxes, remove the water and praise him. He's relaxed when he holds his head at a natural level and ignores the water. Then gradually work the spray up his legs, regularly rewarding quiet behavior and increasing the water pressure as he gains confidence. Repeat on the other side.

Problem-Solving Strategies

- Make sure you use a strong halter and lead to tie. Consider not using a snap or any gimmicks that could send mixed signals to the horse. Don't let your emotions allow techniques that hinder your horse's future training. Don't tie to anything that you suspect could break or pull out of the ground.

- At first your horse might pick up his feet, move around or become excited. Continue spraying; quit only with success. If you quit training every time he resists, you teach him to misbehave.

- Avoid spraying your horse's face and getting water in his ears and nose. Few horses enjoy these sensations, and you want water to be a positive element.

- If your horse kicks at the water with one leg, he's just nervous. Keep spraying until he relaxes. If he kicks at you with one or both feet, this signifies a lack of respect, which I consider inherently dangerous.

117

Seek professional help to cure your disrespectful horse before you get hurt.

- If he pulls back, continue spraying his legs. "Setting back" is an indication that basic training was not performed properly, or by a competent trainer. If you stay out of your horse's danger zone, just the halter pressure encourages him to step up for an immediate reward of no pressure.

2. Make the most of mud. Next, ground-drive your horse through mud puddles in your round pen, exposing him to the slick, soggy footing and strengthening your forward, stop and directional cues. The best way to do that is after it rains, or create your own soggy setup by soaking your pen.

Ground-drive your horse at a walk and a trot until he moves freely and readily responds to your cues. Then advance to a wet arena and eventually to larger puddles outside the pen to further build his confidence and confirm your control.

Problem-Solving Strategies

- If your horse is truly afraid of water, not just unruly, drive him around the puddle, keeping his nose pointed toward it, until he relaxes. If you allow him to circle away from the scary stimuli, he takes advantage of that, escalating the problem.

  Remember: You make the decisions of where and when your horse moves, not him.

- Then gradually move closer to the "monster," as described in Chapter 8, "Ride Through the Fear." Don't try to force your horse into the water. Instead, be patient and just keep working him around the mud puddle. You might make several circles before your horse relaxes, but eventually your horse no longer notices the water and takes that important first step into it.

- Once your horse steps into the puddle, keep him moving straight ahead with your voice and body cues. If you attempt to force him to stop, he focuses on his feet, setting the stage for a panic situation. But, once he relaxes to the point that he stops in the water, give him a rest right there. That is his reward.

- If your horse slips and falls, don't make a big deal of it; consider this a training opportunity. With the right attitude, you can turn little mishaps into confidence-building exercises. Kiss to your horse, loosen your lines and allow him to get up. Once he's up, keep him moving. Horses have fallen down for thousands of years and then continued on. Unless you have allowed a dangerous environment to exist, your horse won't have a problem.

Under-Saddle Solution

1. Reinforce the right response. To keep your horse as calm as possible with you aboard, don't ask for too much too fast, but do get him working. Just as you did in the ground-driving exercise, begin in the round pen, gradually working to an arena and open area, as you and your horse are ready. Before crossing a river, gradually introduce your horse to puddles and shallow streams like the one shown in Photo 1A. If you have been deliberate and consistent with your ground-work cues, you should be set for success in the saddle. The horse in these photos has advanced to being ridden outside the arena, so I demonstrate the following steps on a large water-crossing. Use the same method whether you negotiate a puddle in the round pen or a water-crossing on the trail.

Riding two-handed for direct-rein control, briskly guide your horse toward the middle of the puddle. If he acts alert with his ears and nose pointing forward, feels tense and you suspect he's telling you he's not going to cross, and you merely allow him to work along the edge, he can cheat you. Stay relaxed so you don't inadvertently upset him. Ask him to move forward toward one side of the puddle. Then quietly ask him to turn, still facing the puddle, and walk toward the other side, as I'm doing in Photo 1B. Then quietly ask him to turn back, still facing the puddle, and move toward the other side. Keep him doing this "squashed figure 8" pattern until he focuses on following your directions. Do not pull with two reins. Continue this until, during these turns, his front feet are crossing the puddle. That is when you know he is more focused on responding to your cues to avoid your corrections than he is the puddle. As soon as his front feet are in the water, turn him directly across the puddle. Without hesitation, cross the puddle and continue on. By focusing your horse's attention on your guidance, you reinforce that you're the pilot.

As your horse approaches any obstacle, pick up the pace just a tad. Allow him to lower his head, but immediately start pushing him forward vigorously, rather than allowing him to stop. Stopping only gives him an opportunity to freeze and panic or refuse. Also don't allow him to eat grass. If he's calm enough to think about food, that's a clue he's not too concerned with the water and is accustomed to making decisions for both of you. Instead, use your reins and legs to keep his body moving and his head pointed in the intended direction.

Problem-Solving Strategies

- If your horse is afraid to approach the water, take him to a comfort zone and actively perform familiar maneuvers to encourage him to relax, as I'm doing in Photo 1C. Then gradually move closer to the obstacle, as described in Chapter 8, "Ride Through the Fear." It might take several sessions to get your horse near the water's edge.

- If your horse truly is afraid of water, and you recognize you're about to be overwhelmed, follow a reliable horse across the water. Literally stick your horse's nose into the lead horse's tail for assurance. When your horse is well into the water, allow the other horse to ride ahead so your horse mentally copes with his fear.

- If your horse sidesteps around the puddle, block this evasion by focusing on controlling two things: his face and his feet. Make bit contact with your inside rein, keeping the horse's nose aimed at the water. Use your legs and voice to drive him forward. If he doesn't respond, spank his rump with the ends of your reins for motivation.

  Turning his face without pushing him forward often results in a horse "rubbernecking," i.e., facing the direction you want him to go, but moving laterally, in the opposite direction, sometimes driving your legs into a tree or some other undesirable place.

- If your horse backs up rather than moves sideways, firmly encourage him forward with leg pressure and heel bumps. Pick an entry point into the water when you first see the obstacle. Focus your horse on that point well before he thinks of balking. When he steps forward, reward his effort orally while continuing to ask for another step. Keep in mind: As long as he's moving you're successful. Even backing is better than freezing and then exploding.

- If your horse rears, immediately suspect that you are inadvertently pulling on both reins. Tip: Ask a riding buddy to make sure you don't inadvertently send mixed signals by pulling on both reins. Stay calm, guide your horse with only one rein and continue working toward your goal.

  Caution: Rearing is dangerous behavior. Slow down and figure out what you are doing wrong before you continue, rather than resorting to a tie-down. The latter only adds to the frustration. If necessary, and you feel you can't handle the situation, seek professional training assistance. Your fear only compounds the problem.

2. Get his feet wet. Continue to briskly and persistently direct your horse toward the target—the middle of the crossing. Once your horse commits to the water-crossing,

praise him orally and by staying out of his mouth, as shown in Photo 2, but don't allow him to back out. Use leg pressure and voice cues to keep him moving forward. Support him through the water-crossing with light rein contact.

Initially, your horse might rush through the water. That's okay as long as he crosses through the center; however, don't allow him to drift to one side and only halfway cross the water. That only teaches him that he can get away with quitting—the opposite of the response you want. Use direct-rein and leg pressure to keep him in the center. For example, if he drifts left, lead his nose to the right with your right rein, press your left leg behind the cinch to "close the gate" on movement in that direction, and release your right leg to "open the gate" to movement toward the center of the crossing.

Problem-Solving Strategies
- Be prepared for any reaction from your horse—and to take action. For example, your horse might jump the water. If he

leaps, don't punish him. Instead, stay balanced and loosen your reins. When he lands, praise his efforts and try again. After a few leaps, he becomes more relaxed and his movements become smaller until he quietly moves into the water.

- Remember: The control you seek has two parts—directing the face and driving the feet—and won't succeed without both. Point your horse's face in the direction you want to go and drive him forward. Pointing the face without driving him forward just allows him to drift sideways away from or out of the water.

- Your horse might look at the entry point, but move sideways and follow his shoulder—rubbernecking. In this case, he won't respond to only the follow-his-face cue. You must back up that with firm leg cues to send him in the direction of his nose. Consider not teaching the horse to overflex during training. That may get the rider some temporary control, but when a horse learns to move laterally while his face is looking the other way, the result can be unpleasant and dangerous.

3. Repeat. Once you've passed through the water, reward your horse by riding away

4A

from it and allowing him to relax. Then, approach the water again, polishing his performance. As your horse progresses, weave through the water to further develop his confidence. Repeat until walking through the puddle is uneventful. For some horses this might take a few minutes or an hour; for others it might require several weeks of persistent practice.

Problem-Solving Strategies
- If your horse tries to avoid the water, block his path with the leg on that side and opposite direct-rein pressure. For example, if he tries to escape to the right, press your right

leg against his side, pull his nose to the left with direct-rein pressure and drive him forward. Keep him working and focused on you by continuing the "squashed figure 8" pattern until his front feet are in the water, and then move forward.

4. Expand your horse's horizons. Now, test your horse's confidence on gradually larger water-crossings, such as creeks and rivers. Choose a safe spot to cross and keep his head facing that spot. Opt for a level crossing point or gradual slope with safe, solid footing. A steep, slick drop-off with sharp rocks could shatter the confidence you've worked so hard

4B

to build. Also, for further assurance, enter and exit the water in shallow areas, where your horse can see the bottom and isn't required to swim.

Once your horse relaxes, he might take a drink, as the horse in Photo 4A has. This is okay, but when he starts pawing or becoming restless, drive him through the water. You don't want to risk his becoming excited in a potentially slick area or lying down and rolling with you on his back.

When your horse completes the crossing, repeat from the other side, using the same approach. Practice several times to reinforce that water isn't something to fear. Your persistent practice now prevents future water-crossing worries. In time, your horse even learns to handle obstacles in the water, as shown in Photo 4B.

Problem-Solving Strategies

• Again, if your horse doesn't cross, follow a riding partner with a reliable horse across,

as in Photo 4C, so your horse sees there's nothing to fear. Be careful that this doesn't become a trend. You want your horse to develop the confidence to lead the way.

5. Ponying procedure. For a particularly hesitant horse, have an experienced rider with a familiar, reliable mount pony your horse across the water, as I'm doing with this young packhorse in Photo 5. Practice beforehand in a forgiving environment, such as a sandy round pen without a rider on the trainee for best results and to introduce the horse to what's expected of him. Then work up to introducing a rider wearing a helmet and eventually to ponying across the water.

To prepare for ponying, place a durable halter with lead over the bridle. Retain the reins as you're ponied, just in case something goes wrong and you need control. The rider ahead should dally (wrap), not tie, the lead rope a couple of times around the saddle horn until the fearful horse is near the rider's

4C

knee. This allows the rider control of the horse should he become excited, and it allows the rider to release the rope if things get out of hand. When ponying a horse, use the same mindset as when tying a horse. You don't want the trainee to pull loose or you teach the wrong lesson.

Problem-Solving Strategies
• Don't allow anyone to pony you unless you know the person and his or her horse well, and trust his or her ponying abilities.

Occasionally a frustrated horse can lunge forward to the point his front feet are in the pony horse's saddle. For most folks, it's much safer to follow a seasoned horse into the water than to pony a fearful mount.

• If your horse has been taught that it is okay to pull when tied, or when being led, ponying is not an appropriate technique until you fix this problem. See Chapter 5, "Never a Fit to be Tied," to improve your horse's response to pressure.

KINSEY'S KEYS TO SUCCESS

- **Work out playfulness.** To burn your horse's excess energy, so he focuses on you and gets into a learning mindset, longe or work him in a round pen before you train.

- **Settle only for success.** Train your horse to cross water in simple, sequential steps he understands, rewarding his slightest efforts and ending on a positive note. Rather than place a time limit on training, take all the time necessary to achieve the smallest success.

- **Keep your cool.** If you don't make a big deal of things, your horse senses your confidence and is less likely to become excited.

- **Call the shots.** Before you attempt water-crossings, make sure your horse approaches obstacles without a fight. Then encourage him to cross water with the instructions outlined in this chapter. To do so, your horse must respect your authority, control and guidance.

- **Practice consistency.** Direct your horse to the center of every water-crossing or obstacle. If you allow your horse to move around the obstacle, you're not paying attention, and he decides what he wants to do and when to cooperate.

- **Use good judgment.** Recognize when obstacles are outside your and your horse's capabilities. Attempting and failing is detrimental to your and your horse's confidence, and your training program.

- **Forego whips and spurs.** Misuse could frighten your horse and tarnish past and future training efforts. Instead, rely on consistent, persistent training techniques based on trust and respect.

- **Safety first.** If you feel out of control or in danger, stop and seek help from a professional horseman before you compromise your or your horse's safety.

Learn how to traverse various trail terrain with proper horsemanship and common sense.

12

RIDING IN THE ROUGH

If you've watched a fair share of westerns, you've observed cowboys galloping horses up and down mountainsides and craggy bluffs, trailing the herd or outlaws. Your stomach sinks as the camera pans the action. The movie-star horsemen make riding in rough terrain appear effortless, and so can you.

Although you probably don't need to hit the trail hard and fast, you should know how to traverse varied terrain in the safest manner for you and your horse. In this section, I cover fundamental horsemanship and safety guidelines when riding up and down hills, and on such difficult footing as rocks and ice.

To negotiate rough terrain, your horse must have the following skills:

• Move forward, backward and stop readily.

- Yield laterally in both directions to direct-rein pressure.

- Accept your authority and direction willingly.

- Remain calm and dependable in various riding conditions.

- Collect his body on cue. This is beneficial, but not required.

Terrain Types

1. Uphill. Most trails have inclines, whether rolling hills or steep mountain slopes, so you must know how to guide your horse up and down hills in the easiest, most efficient way possible. However, climbing hills is difficult for a horse, and packing a rider makes it even more challenging. To perform hill work correctly, your horse must develop the strength and coordination necessary to distribute his weight on his hindquarters to push himself uphill. To aid the horse, you should remain centered, as weight shifts interfere with his balance and movement, causing missteps.

Rider position: For a solid base of support, press most of your weight into the stirrups, keeping your heels level with your toes. To help stabilize your torso, grip from the knees up. Lean forward slightly, keeping your upper body vertical and parallel with the trees around you and your rear end lightly contacting the saddle. If you're in a treeless area, keep in mind that trees typically grow vertically, regardless of the terrain's slope, and you should be vertical, too. Your body position shouldn't deviate much from that of the trees, no matter the terrain; just adjust to allow the horse and saddle to change angles beneath you. Help your horse by staying balanced over his center of gravity, roughly the front-cinch area. Keep your shoulders square, as in Photo 1A, and look ahead so you don't fall forward.

Hold your reins with enough slack that your horse can use his head and neck for balance, but not so loosely that you can't establish instant contact with his mouth if needed.

1A

If you feel unbalanced, momentarily grab a handful of mane or the horn to stabilize yourself. However, avoid leaning backward because that causes you to apply pressure to the reins and risks pulling your horse backward on top of you. If you stay balanced, with your legs and body vertical, you don't pull on the saddle horn or mane. As a rule, don't sacrifice control for the saddle horn.

Horse position: Keep your horse's nose pointed uphill, as in Photo 1B, using leg pressure rather than the reins to avoid moving his face when climbing. Adjust your horse's head as little as possible to maximize his balance. However, be ready to use direct-rein pressure, if necessary, to insist he climb uphill and remain facing in that direction.

On steep inclines, don't let your horse turn. A horse isn't stable standing sideways on a steep slope; his feet easily can slip out from under him, and young horses or horses unable to manage a rider's weight can topple.

To discourage your horse from turning, drive him straight uphill by assuming proper position, squeezing his sides with your legs and kissing to him. If he's reluctant to move or shows signs of wanting to turn around, spank his rump with the ends of your reins.

Young or novice horses usually rush uphill because they haven't developed the mental discipline, strength and coordination to handle the incline. Although it's safest to walk uphill, strive for success initially and then refine your horse's technique as he becomes comfortable. As discussed in the chapter on crossing obstacles, it's better for a horse to rush through the terrain initially, as long as he moves uphill, than to have him become frustrated and refuse to move. Reward your horse with rest.

Once your horse realizes he can handle the hill, practice moving at the pace you want. If you allow your horse to pick the pace, he quickly learns it's okay to gain momentum whenever he wants, setting the stage for a dangerous situation. To slow your horse, use one rein or alternating-rein pressure, depending on how your horse is trained. If you pull on both reins, you risk pulling a fussy or frustrated horse over on top of you.

Problem-Solving Strategies
- Start your horse with gentle inclines and small rises. Just as a workhorse or roping horse needs to begin with small loads to build confidence, the young or novice trail horse does, as well. Pushing a young or novice horse into too much too early can cause him to become frustrated.

- If your horse attempts to stop, use the cues outlined above to get him moving. If needed, pop his rump with your rein ends to let him know that you mean for him to go now. If your horse freezes, you failed to "listen" to him and anticipate the impending problem. If you fail to recognize his frustration, his need to rest or his pain, and push him until he quits, you've initiated an annoying and dangerous problem.

1B

2A

You want the horse to move and stop only when you ask.

- If your horse is offering his best effort and becomes tired, it's okay to lead him uphill. However, keep in mind that on really steep, slippery slopes, a decent rider is safer in the saddle than under the horse's feet. To safely lead your horse, stay several feet in front of him, leading him with a long rein or two reins snapped together.

2. Downhill. Negotiating downhill terrain is actually more dangerous than uphill inclines because any interference or misstep could cause your horse to topple headfirst, flinging you over his head and beneath him. Riding downhill also requires a lot more rider control than riding uphill does, and your horse must have hindquarters strength and balance to reach far under himself with his hind legs. If your horse isn't reliable or responsive to your cues, or hasn't developed these skills, establish that control and collection before you attempt hill work.

Rider position: Use similar body position while riding downhill as you do uphill—balanced, upright and parallel to the trees. Shift your seat back slightly and push against the stirrups, with your heels level with your toes, to avoid falling forward. Relative to the horse and saddle, you appear to be leaning back. Don't lean too far back into a water-skiing-like position, however, or you're behind your horse's motion, thus at risk for him to leave you in the dust if he suddenly spooks or bolts. Grip from the knees up, keeping weight in the stirrups to maintain lateral and vertical stability. Relax and move with the horse to stay balanced, as shown in Photo 2A.

As with riding uphill, leave enough slack in your reins for your horse to use his natural balance, but also maintain enough control that you can support him down the hill and rate his speed.

Horse position: Keep your horse facing downhill, rather than allowing him to turn sideways. If he loses his footing while sideways, he's likely to fall, putting you in a vulnerable position. On the other hand, if his

2B

NECESSARY EQUIPMENT

- **Bridle with a smooth-mouthed snaffle bit, chin strap (bit hobble) and split reins.** All of these allow you to guide your horse with direct-rein pressure, enhancing your control. A correctly adjusted chin strap prevents pulling the bit through the horse's mouth.

- **Saddle and blanket or pad.** Avoid excessively thick pads that require excessive tightening or might allow the saddle to slip when riding up- and downhill.

- **Breast collar.** To further stabilize your saddle, use a breast-collar with a center strap that attaches to your front cinch.

- **Breeching or crupper.** If your horse is mutton-withered (has low withers) or just doesn't carry a saddle well, help stabilize your saddle when going downhill with breeching or a crupper. Accustom your horse to the gear in the round pen before you hit the trail. Pulling the crupper under his tail or breeching around his rear end might startle him at first.

- **Helmets.** Although I'm not wearing a helmet in these photos, I recommend and do wear one in questionable situations and on problem horses.

nose points downhill, he can shift his weight onto his hindquarters when he slides and regain his balance.

For safety and to prevent joint stress and injuries, walk your horse downhill, encouraging him to collect. This causes him to distribute his weight onto his hindquarters, lightening his front end so he can step without stumbling.

Problem-Solving Strategies

- Make sure you have complete control and clear communication with your horse before negotiating downhill terrain. This is not the place to discover just how poorly controlled or passive-aggressive your horse is, or just how badly you can get hurt.

- Start on small embankments, 2- or 3-foot slopes, as shown in Photo 2B. Successfully negotiate a hill a few times and end on a positive note, rather than drilling your horse to frustration and boredom. Repeat for a few more lessons, or until your horse is confident and you have complete control. Then advance to 4- to 5-foot inclines and higher in the same manner.

- Often, a horse balks at downhill obstacles. If that happens, first make sure you're not

causing the problem by tensing—a common problem at the beginning of the obstacles. If you're not at fault, your horse is calling the shots. Regain control by applying your go-forward cues with authority until he moves. Then reward his effort by allowing him to go without fussing.

- Instill good habits in your horse by always making him walk downhill. Don't allow young riders or inexperienced or unsafe riding partners to set bad examples for your horse by jogging their horses down the slope in front of you. This is a dangerous, distracting habit.

- If your horse tries to trot or lope downhill, either he hasn't developed the self-discipline, balance and strength to negotiate the slope in a collected manner, or he's making the decisions for you. In the first instance, continue to perform regular hill work to increase your horse's coordination and conditioning. For the latter, turn around, walk back up the hill and ask your horse to walk down it. Repeat as often as necessary to ingrain the right response, rewarding his progress.

3. Rocky footing. From gravel roads to craggy canyons, rocks are unavoidable when trail riding. If not traversed properly, though, rocky terrain can cause your horse to slip or stumble, or bruise the soles of his feet.

Rider position: If you're riding up- or downhill, assume the same positions outlined in the previous sections and as shown in Photo 3A. Balanced body position helps your horse to stay balanced across the rocks.

Hold your reins in the same manner outlined above, but be ready to quickly give slack if your horse jerks his nose down to compensate for a painful step. Jerking his mouth, even inadvertently, is poor horsemanship, and violates the horse's trust. To prevent pulling on his mouth or falling forward if he stumbles, ride with your index finger and thumb forming an O around the reins. That way, if you must grab the reins, you can, but the reins don't jerk through your hands for about 6 inches before you close the O.

Horse position: Move through rocky ground at a walk, allowing your horse to pick his path. He'll carry his head lower than normal, so allow plenty of rein slack. If he picks his way off the trail, use leg and direct

3A

pressure to guide him back on track before he slams you into trees and branches. Giving slack does not mean giving up control.

Aid your horse by directing him in a controlled manner around large or sharp rocks, as in Photo 3B. Use direct-rein and leg pressure to guide him efficiently. If you need to cross large slick rock surfaces, remain balanced with two hands on the reins and focus on slowly guiding your horse. This isn't the place to play balancing games, as your horse could fall and suffer a career-ending injury.

Problem-Solving Strategies
- Apply the principles and techniques outlined in the other terrain types.

4. Ice. It's best to avoid riding in icy conditions to prevent injuring you or your horse. However, if you inadvertently find yourself on a slippery spot, take precautions to make sure you and your horse make it across safely.

Rider position: Balance over your horse's center of gravity by shifting your weight onto your inner thighs and stirrups, as described for hill work. If your horse slips, this offers him the best chance of recovering his balance. Remain still and look up and ahead to avoid any interfering with your horse's movement or balance.

Ride with a relatively loose rein so your horse can use his balancing mechanism and see where to walk.

Horse position: First look for a way around the icy spot, especially if it's sloped. If you must cross it, lead your horse as previously described, taking the shortest path possible and encouraging him to take small, cautious steps.

Problem-Solving Strategies
- If your horse slips, slow down and stay calm. If he's young, scared and shaking, ease up to him and rub his neck and shoulder to assure him. Then walk forward and encourage him to follow. Stay far enough away that he can't fall on you or hit you with his feet if he slips.

KINSEY'S KEYS TO SUCCESS

- **Don't expect too much.** Consider the ride's duration, the weight your horse is carrying, his conditioning and his confidence. Avoid asking your horse to do more than he's capable of doing, or he could become sore or injured. Also, if you take your horse into terrain you're not comfortable with, you could get into a dangerous situation that violates the trust you've worked so hard to build. Initially, opt for mild terrain, gradually advancing to more rugged country. My assistants and I condition our trail horses at a nearby abandoned railroad embankment, directing the horses up and down slopes varying from 2 to 20 feet.

- **Monitor your horse.** If he heaves heavily and his sides drip with sweat, slow down—you're pushing too hard. If you push your horse past his limit, he can become so fatigued that he starts to refuse to work and could injure himself.

- **Look ahead.** Observing upcoming obstacles and difficult terrain allows you to plan and prepare for success.

- **Find a farrier.** Before you ride in rocky areas, shoe your horse appropriately for increased traction and to reduce the risk of stone bruises and other hoof injuries.

- **Keep your cool.** If you're confident and don't make a big deal out of things, you reassure your horse, increasing his responsiveness and obedience.

- **Give your horse freedom.** As your horse works through difficult terrain, he needs his head and neck to balance. Tie-downs, short roping reins, heavy bits, mechanical hackamores and other gimmicks only restrict his balance. If you've followed my training series and have practiced using leg cues and draped reins with a snaffle bit, your backcountry experience will be much easier and less frustrating for you and your horse.

- **Boost your balance.** Your balance and overall physical fitness can help or hinder your horse. If you remain centered and upright in the saddle, your horse doesn't have to compensate for your weight shifts. Conversely, if you don't have the strength to stabilize your body, your horse must step in the direction you move to remain balanced. To put this in perspective, imagine that someone is riding on your shoulders. If that person leans, you must do the same to prevent tipping over.

- **Stay "on top" of the situation.** In most situations it's best to try to stay on your horse if he falls, or at least get away from his feet to prevent getting stepped on or kicked. If you fall off, immediately become aware of the horse's movement and get out of the way so he doesn't run over you and cause further damage. Also, don't allow him to run away while you assess your injuries, exposing your horse to more danger. Instead, calmly catch him or have a helper do so.

- **Teach patience.** Horses that have been taught to stand patiently are less likely to hurt you or struggle when unexpected falls or tangles occur. Just as we introduce our foals to restraint by initially holding them, we teach our trail horses to stand tied for a couple of hours and to accept hobbles. Such training pays big dividends when the unexpected occurs. Helplessly watching a horse thrash around and injure himself because he hasn't been taught patience makes a believer out of any novice horse owner.

Control your horse's "I won't do this" attitude with this simple solution.

13

TRAIL TANTRUMS

Does your horse jig, balk or even spin around and bolt back to the barn or trailer when you ride him away? If so, he's barn-sour, and his tantrums are not only annoying, but also dangerous. I've watched riders fall off as their horses ran to the barn or spun violently. I've also seen horses carry their riders into brush and trees, run into gates, bolt onto busy roads and slam into other horses, in turn unseating other riders.

Here, I tell you what causes barn-sour behavior and how you can break it for good by developing the skills you need to get your horse to respect your go-forward cues. Before your horse can understand this fix, he should have the following foundations skills:

NECESSARY EQUIPMENT

- **Halter and lead rope.** I use a hand-tied rope halter with a 12-foot lead on most mares or geldings and a 20-foot lead on stallions and hard-to-handle horses for more control.

- **Bridle with smooth-mouthed snaffle bit and chin strap (bit hobble).** This bit allows you to ride two-handed and guide your horse's nose in the direction you want. Secure a chin strap to the rings to prevent pulling the bit through your horse's mouth. Adjust the strap so you can fit only two fingers between the strap and your horse's chin.

- **Saddle and blanket.** It's also a good idea to use a breast collar and properly adjusted rear cinch to help

keep the saddle in place. Avoid thick pads or flexible saddles that need cinching tightly to stay in place. Too much padding can cause equine discomfort and saddle slippage.

- **Round pen.** For safety, I prefer a 60-foot round pen with soft ground and 6-foot high, durable, horse-safe panels. Make sure your enclosure is also free of sharp edges or obstacles that could injure you or your horse.

- **35-foot driving lines.** See Chapter 7 for information on driving lines.

- **Gloves.** It's a good idea to don gloves to protect your hands, although I'm not doing so in these photos.

- Longes under control.

- Yields to direct-rein pressure in both directions.

- Moves forward, backward and stops readily in response to your leg, voice and rein cues. There's a difference between a horse that moves because it's convenient for him to move and one that moves because he respects and understands your requests. The latter is your goal.

What's Behind Barn-Sour Behavior?

Understanding the basis for barn-sour behavior helps you correct and prevent the problem. I believe barn-sour behavior is taught through rewards, while herd-bound behavior is an instinctual issue we cover later in the next chapter. Ask any horseman if he's had an untrained or green horse run back to the barn or trailer. I suspect the answer is no. Sure, such horses might run past the barn, maybe to the pasture or paddock, or perhaps to a herd, but most untrained horses don't have an affinity with the barn or trailer. We teach our horses that the barn or trailer is a place of relaxation and reward by unsaddling them and turning them loose when we get there.

Horses become barn-sour in two ways: first, by what we actively do and, second, by what we don't do. The first is the most difficult to retrain or might never be satisfactorily retrained. Due to a lack of control and communication, some riders find that the easiest situation in which to get a horse to

lope is when going back to the barn or trailer. Your horse picks up this unintentional lesson quickly. He learns that if he gets to the barn as fast as he can, he gets rid of his tack and trainer so he can hang out with his buddies and eat. That's why it's best to walk your horse to the barn or trailer, or loosen the cinch in a random spot and lead him there. That way, he doesn't associate the reward of quitting with the barn or trailer.

An example of the second way of learning is when you don't control your horse and allow him to turn toward the barn without being directed to do so. Allowing this is the first step in developing barn-sour behavior. Ask yourself whether he's doing what you asked him to do, or what you're allowing him to do.

Increasing your control, thus safety, starts in the round pen. When your horse complies with your cues there, advance to a larger pen, arena and eventually, short trail rides.

Recognize the Signs

Barn-sour behavior is akin to a spoiled child stomping his feet, shaking his fist and screaming, "I won't do this!" As with a child, such behavior, if ignored, worsens with time. The key to solving the behavior: Recognize such pre-tantrum signals and establish your horse's respect early on in your relationship.

On his turf or in a group, a barn-sour horse might be quiet and reliable. In fact, many riders depend on the group for control, rather than developing control from the start, and might not recognize barn-sour signs. When you ask your horse to leave the barn or trailer, his conditioned response kicks in and his goal becomes getting home. As he jigs along the trail, he tunes you out, becomes disobedient and pushes through the bit. His head and tail raise, and he fixes his eyes and ears on home. You feel him tense and shorten his stride until he stops, refuses to move and even rears. He might also suddenly spin around and bolt back to the barn or trailer.

Simple Solution

Solving barn- or trailer-sour behavior is simple, if you realize it's a people problem. The solution involves gaining your horse's respect and obedience from the ground, and then in the saddle.

1. Lead your horse away from the barn or trailer. This elementary step helps build his respect, particularly if he's developed barn-sour behavior since you've had him. Outfit your horse in a halter and appropriate lead. Lead him from the barn or trailer until he starts to show signs of disobedience. The distance varies for each horse and lesson. Keep him at that spot for 10 to 15 minutes, longe-ing him in both directions until he obeys your requests. Longeing not only helps gain his attention and respect, but it also removes nervous energy that hinders training.

As your horse develops respect, gradually lead him father away, out of sight of the barn. Then longe him and keep him there up to 30 minutes. Repeat until you have his full cooperation anywhere you go.

Problem-Solving Strategies

• If your horse pulls back, move with him to avoid a tug-of-war. When he stops, firmly bump the lead backward to make him back a few steps further. This reinforces the notion that you're in control, not him.

• If your horse tries to get ahead of you, firmly bump the rope backward a few times to slow him down.

• If your horse becomes willful, be assertive to let him know that complying with your cues is easier than defying them. Here's an example: If he won't willingly lead, immediately longe him around you until he

moves willingly. Then ask him to lead again. If he longes a flat-sided circle, veering toward the barn on one side and nearly running over you on the "far" side from the barn, tip his nose to the inside of the circle with line pressure, and encourage him to do the assigned task properly. It might take several repetitions, but he learns that it's much easier to lead willingly than to longe.

2. Ground-drive your horse. Ingrain into your horse that he's to move and stop on command, not when it's convenient for him, by ground-driving him in a round pen, as shown in Photo 2. When he complies with your cues, progress to a larger pen, arena, the barn area, and then wide-open spaces. Repeat until you have complete control, indicating the respect and obedience you need to have.

3. Ride in an enclosed area. When you're ready to ride, begin in the safety of a round pen if possible. For this chapter, I'm on the trail, so have chosen the safe, level area in Photo 3 to school my horse. Your goal is cooperation, and you achieve that through respect and understanding. Be an active rider, asking your horse to perform combinations of maneuvers, such as turns in both directions and serpentines, interspersed with speed transitions, stops and backs. This develops control

and responsiveness, plus it takes his mind off the barn. Use your seat, legs and kiss cue to send your horse forward, and encourage him to yield to lateral direct-rein pressure. These are key elements to keep him moving on the trail. Avoid overworking him; otherwise, you exacerbate his barn-sour problem. Instead, work toward success, not to a set time on your watch. When you make any progress toward your goal, reward him. Get off at a random spot, loosen your cinch and lead him to the point where you can unsaddle and put him up.

Practice until your horse works in a relaxed, responsive manner, and keep in mind it might take multiple sessions. When you're confident in your control, advance to an arena, around the barn area and, eventually, the trail.

4. Expand your riding range. Mount up and gradually ride farther from your horse's familiar environment. Your goal is to maintain forward motion and keep his nose tipped away from the barn, so avoid stopping, turning or other delays. Be ready to make him do what you want, remaining calm and confident, and direct with your cues so you don't transfer tension or cause confusion. Ride two-handed for direct-rein control, and use your natural aids to signal him to walk or trot.

3

It's often easier to encourage a horse to move away from the barn at a jog than a walk. Ask him to serpentine and perform speed transitions, to keep him focused on you, rather than home. Ride until he calms down, then dismount, loosen your cinch and lead him back to the barn.

With each lesson, ride him farther away from home until he's reliable and responsive anywhere.

Problem-Solving Strategies

- Ride your horse through his nervousness if he gets edgy. If you don't have the area to get away, ride him back to a previous comfort zone. Work him there until he cooperates, and then again slowly expand the distance.

- If your horse stops and/or attempts to turn and head back to the barn or trailer, use

4

direct-rein pressure to keep his nose pointed away from home. I call this "cue and correct." The cue is the light directional pull of the rein, and the correction is a bump with the same rein. Execute the cue and correction in the same tempo as it takes to say, "Cue and correct." The more determined your horse becomes in having his way, the more assertive you need to be. Point his nose in the direction you want to go and drive him forward. If he gets his way and heads back to the barn, return to the leading and driving exercises to establish control and obedience.

- If your horse pokes his nose forward or in the opposite direction you want, this is a blatant sign of disobedience. Correct him immediately, firmly directing his nose in the correct direction with direct-rein pressure. Encourage him to flex to the point you can see the edge of his eye and nostril, as in Photo 4; if you flex his neck any farther, you impede forward motion. Back up your rein cues with your legs and voice to encourage him to follow his nose. When he yields to the pressure and moves, reward him with pressure release.

- If you feel overwhelmed or need a break, secure a halter over your bridle. Tie your horse at or above withers level to a sturdy post away from the barn, and allow him to throw his tantrums until he's done. When he stands quietly, mount and start training again. This lets him know that you determine when to return to the barn. With time, patience and adequate persuasion you take care of your horse's trail tantrums for good, and develop a willing trail partner.

Pilot Errors
- **Pilot Pitfall A:** Overflexing your horse. Resist the urge to crank your horse's head to your knee or circle him in this situation. All too often overflexing becomes a "rest" reward for misbehavior. Commonly an overflexed, frustrated horse bites a rider's foot or leg. Occasionally a horse learns to "rubberneck," i.e. move his body the direction he wants to go while flexed to the rider's knee. Rubbernecking is a dangerous lesson for a horse to learn. Turning the horse around allows him to think about going home. Instead, use your direct rein to tip his nose away from the barn or trailer, and use your legs and voice to drive him forward.

- **Pilot Pitfall B:** Pulling back, or being "in" your horse's mouth. Sometimes a rider panics and, without realizing it, maintains steady backward pressure on the reins, frustrating the horse. Not only does this

A

send mixed signals, but your horse also probably tries to escape the pressure by raising his head and sticking out his nose. You also risk him running backward or rearing. In time, he learns to brace against pressure, not a characteristic of a reliable trail mount.

- **Pilot Pitfall C:** Using gimmicks. Some riders try to develop control through gimmicks, such as severe bits and tie-downs. This often indicates that the rider has abandoned his training responsibility, substituting force and pain. For a trail horse to negotiate myriad obstacles on the trail, he needs maximum mobility. Tie-downs and other devices hinder mobility. Use of severe bits too often can result in a horse coming over backward on a rider.

- **Pilot Pitfall D:** Neck-reining nonsense. I consider neck-rein and verbal cues easily ignored requests. I appreciate them and teach them, but I also recognize that a horse can easily ignore them in stressful situations. If you try to neck-rein a poorly trained or uncooperative horse, you fail

to gain control. Use defensive-riding techniques, that is, a direct rein in each hand when issues arise.

- **Pilot Pitfall E:** Getting personal. Too many folks take a horse's rebellion personally. Some riders opt to solve problems with abuse, while others look for loving solutions. Neither is appropriate. Instead of getting mad or taking things personally, be firm yet fair, and seek help from a qualified trainer if necessary.

- **Pilot Pitfall F:** Misusing whips and spurs. Riders who are in over their heads often resort to whips and spurs, and they're a short-term solution. Whips and spurs used by a struggling rider can result in an ugly confrontation that could get you hurt. Furthermore, misusing them could cause your horse to buck you off and bolt to the barn. If that happens you could get hurt, plus you might have taught him that bucking is a great way to get back to the barn. If you feel as though you need to rely on whips and spurs, go back to the basics, and get help if necessary.

KINSEY'S KEYS TO SUCCESS

- **Recognize the reason.** Resolving barn-sour behavior is different for a horse that acts out of willful disobedience than for one that's afraid or insecure. This exercise isn't appropriate for a fearful horse and could do more harm than good. If you can't recognize the difference, ask a qualified horseman for help.

- **Identify your influence.** Did your horse have this problem when you bought him? If not, you might've taught him this habit. You need to understand how you influenced the problem, and how you can avoid making the problem worse.

- **Be an involved rider.** Building on the previous point, each time you ride, you train your horse, whether you instill good or bad habits. Your horse doesn't understand good or bad. Instead he decides what's easiest and most comfortable for him. Decide what you want your horse to learn and make it happen.

- **Cooperate with your horse.** You and your horse can accomplish much more with cooperation, rather than force. If you fight with your horse, more times than not he wins. The barn-sour horse already has won enough times to realize it's easier to bully his way to the barn than to carry you around.

- **Encourage cooperation.** Remember, your horse does whatever is easiest for him. My methods put him in situations that allow you to make him uncomfortable when he's disobedient, so he learns that it's easier to cooperate and comply with your cues.

- **Use common sense.** If you feel as though you and your horse are in danger, or if you get frightened or uncomfortable, seek help from a knowledgeable horseman.

- **Allow plenty of time and patience.** Building your horse's confidence away from his comfort zone can take any amount of time, depending on his training and willingness, and you must reward the slightest effort. Expecting too much too soon or using force causes confusion and frustration. Work your horse in 10- to 20-minute increments, especially if he's a youngster with a short attention span. Practice daily, gradually increasing the difficulty as he's ready, until he readily responds to your requests. Shortcuts often cause confusion or a fight, create other problems or spoil your chances of success.

- **Use precise cues.** Concise, consistent cues send your horse clear messages that, with repetition, he learns to understand.

Does your horse panic whenever his buddy disappears on the trail? Here's how to alleviate your horse's herd-bound behavior.

14

SEPARATION ANXIETY

You and a friend are enjoying a relaxing trail ride...until your friend rides her horse over a hill, out of sight. Your horse tenses and panics, snorting, prancing, shaking his head and nickering frantically. Chomping and pulling on the bit, he feels as though he might bolt at any moment.

If your horse gets nervous whenever his buddy rides away, you're not alone. This is a common, natural behavior in herd animals like horses. However, if his anxiety gets out of hand, a pleasant ride can turn into a disaster. Before either of you gets hurt, you'd be wise to gradually accustom him to riding solo. In this chapter, I tell you what causes herd-bound behavior and how to build your horse's confidence through a series of short separations, where you focus his attention on you, rather than

Your horse instinctively wants to be with his buddies, so it's important to redirect his attention with a training exercise, rather than punish him.

another horse. Before asking him to move away from his pal, he must willingly perform these basic skills:

- Move forward, backward and stop readily in response to your natural aids (hands, legs, voice and seat).

- Yield laterally to direct-rein pressure in both directions.

An Instinctual Issue

Before you handle your horse's herd-bound behavior, it's important to understand why he panics when separated from his friend and how to gradually introduce him to independence.

Herd-bound behavior is instinctual. Your horse evolved as a prey and herd animal, and his ancestors relied on their herd mates for survival. So, when you're on the trail, it's only natural that your horse wants to stick with his buddy for safety.

The same feelings of insecurity and vulnerability to ambush are rooted in horses that resist being the lead or rear horses. Your horse feels as though he's a prime target for predators if he's in the front or rear of the herd.

Because separation anxiety is instinctual behavior, don't punish your horse during training sessions, or you escalate the problem. Instead, train firmly but quietly, trying new techniques gradually to enhance communication with him, and rewarding the slightest effort to build confidence and trust. It is important to keep the horse working and learning so he does not have time to be distracted by his insecurity.

Before we jump into the lesson, here are some things to help gradually accustom your horse to separation, which you can do daily or when you're not riding. Work your horse by himself in a round pen or while ground-

1

driving in an arena or other controlled environment. Keep him in a stall or pen, away from his buddies, during feeding time and through the night. Whatever you do, your training should address two issues: teaching the horse confidence in your judgment, and obeying your directions despite stress or fear. Doing so helps develop a willing, trusting team effort between you and your horse.

Simple Solution
1. Ride together. Ask a friend with a solid, seasoned horse to ride with you and help build your horse's confidence. Walk in a relaxed manner alongside the other rider. Your horse should remain quiet, because he's in his comfort zone.

2. Jog ahead. Riding two-handed, with your hands at saddle-horn level, establish a jog. Jog ahead for three minutes, with your partner continuing to walk. This encourages your horse to

move on his own in short intervals, letting him know that separation isn't permanent.

Jog in serpentines, as though you're pole bending, to focus your horse's attention on you. Bring your inside rein slightly toward the same-side hip to guide his nose in the direction you're headed. For example, to move him to the left, gently pull your left rein toward your left hip. Drive him forward with leg and verbal cues. Once you establish front-end movement the hind end will follow if you don't allow him to hesitate or balk. Simultaneously move your inside leg away from his side, "opening the door" to movement in that direction, and pressing your opposite leg against his side, behind the front cinch to push him left and "close the door" for right-hand movement.

The instant your horse gives his nose and moves in the direction you want, release your pressure to reward him. Allow him to take about five free steps for a reward, then reverse your cues and guide him in the opposite direction. Continue to zigzag in this fashion, taking his mind off his buddy and keeping your horse attuned to you. As he improves, increase the reward time to about 10 steps before asking him to move laterally again.

Problem-Solving Strategies

- Your horse might not willingly leave his companion and comfort zone. Persistently cue him to briskly jog or trot away. Walking allows him enough time to fuss with you. Keep in mind he'll do one of two things: what you make him do, or what you allow

him to do. The first choice is your goal, but avoid asking him to do something you aren't prepared or able to enforce. Otherwise, you teach him to ignore you.

- If your horse stops and/or attempts to turn back toward his buddy, maintain your direct-rein pressure with one rein to keep his nose pointed in the direction you want him to go, and use leg pressure to drive your horse forward. If necessary, reinforce your cues with a bump on the direct rein or pop his hip with the end of the reins to encourage him forward.

2

• If your horse bolts back to his buddy or throws a tantrum, including rearing and bucking, which scares you and makes you want to quit, you've impeded the training sequence in one of two ways: Either you didn't have your horse's ground-driving and round-pen basics mastered before you advanced to riding, or you overestimated your ability and confidence. In both circumstances your horse takes control, and you've not only perpetuated the problem, you've also compounded it. Return to the basics and practice the ground-driving exercise outlined in Chapter 7 until you know you're in control. Again, if you question your or your horse's safety at any point, get help from a knowledgeable horse person to avoid making the problem worse.

• If you perform these problem-solving strategies and your horse still throws tantrums, you might need to revisit round-pen training techniques. These exercises aren't about making the horse move in circles, but rather about helping the horse recognize you're the "lead horse," not him. This misunderstanding and the resulting lack of respect from your horse are common problems.

3. Ride back and pass your riding partner. Turn and walk back to your oncoming part-

ner, but continue to serpentine as instructed in Step 2. This lets your horse know that separation isn't permanent, and keeps him from rushing back to his buddy—a dangerous habit you want to avoid. If the serpentine isn't enough to maintain control, simply move in circles until your partner catches up. Pass your partner by a small distance, about a horse length initially and more as your horse gains confidence, before turning to follow. This reinforces that riding alone isn't so bad.

Problem-Solving Strategies
• If your horse becomes anxious, maintain control of his mind and body by walking serpentines or small circles.

• If he balks, establish forward motion by turning him and driving him forward with your legs. Then begin to serpentine.

4. Follow your partner. After meeting and riding past your partner, turn before your horse has a chance to get excited and follow your partner for a few steps. You'll feel your horse start to slow down or get anxious, and that's when you should turn and walk behind the other rider. This simply reinforces that you're in charge, not him. Your horse will most likely walk faster than your partner's horse to catch up, but that's okay as long as your horse is listening to you.

153

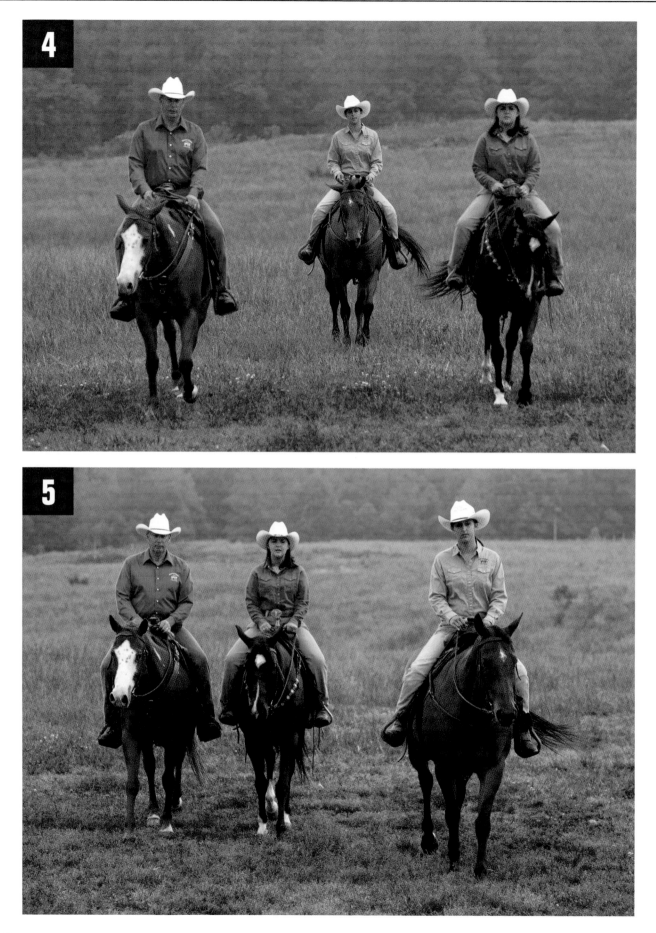

Allow the horses to ride together again as a reward, except this time follow your partner. Your horse will most likely be calm and relieved to have returned to the security of his friend, but continue to serpentine so he doesn't fixate on the other horse's tail. Remember to reward positive response with a few steps of release between requests.

5. Jog ahead. When your horse walks consistently behind your partner, move in front of the other horse, continuing to serpentine and reward between requests. As soon as your horse begins "dragging" and doesn't step out, or wants to turn to the rear horse, repeat this "leapfrog" maneuver several times, until your horse responds to your cues, moves without hesitation and strikes off willingly. Then gradually increase the separation span one minute at a time, working up to short disappearances from sight, such as riding around a bush or in a grove of trees. In the advanced stages, ask for stops, circles, changes of gait or other maneuver to further focus his attention on you, rather than his vanishing partner.

Note that the horse appears more relaxed and confident in Photo 5 than in Photo 2.

Here he's carrying his head in a natural position, and his ears are pointed forward, indicating he's focusing ahead, rather than on the horses behind him. This is the disposition you seek in a dependable trail mount.

Problem-Solving Strategies
- If your horse becomes so anxious that your control is threatened, you might be progressing too quickly. Slow down and return to a previous level until he resumes jogging with confidence. It's important that you recognize when you reach the edge of your horse's comfort zone, or the edge of your skill level, and turn back before losing control.

- Your horse might balk. If he does, establish forward motion by turning him and driving him actively with your legs. Then begin to serpentine.

6. Stop. As your horse masters the leapfrog exercise, increase the difficulty by periodically stopping him, allowing your partner to ride ahead or catch up. Halt your horse with light backward pressure-and-release motion

6A

NECESSARY EQUIPMENT

- **Bridle with a smooth-mouthed snaffle bit, chin strap (bit hobble) and split reins.** All of these allow you to ride defensively two-handed and apply pressure for added control, avoiding confusion. Save neck-reining until your horse is a solid, consistent mount. Secure a chin strap to the rings to prevent pulling the bit through your horse's mouth. Adjust the strap so you can fit only two fingers between the strap and your horse's chin. Attach the reins behind the chin strap and to the snaffle rings.

- **Saddle and blanket.** Avoid thick pads or flexible saddles that need to be cinched tightly to stay in place. Too much padding can cause equine discomfort and saddle slippage. I also use a properly adjusted breast collar and rear cinch to stabilize the saddle.

- **Experienced riding partner with quiet, obedient horse.**

on the reins. Encourage him to stand still and look the opposite direction of his buddy. That way he learns not to fixate on the other horse.

Problem-Solving Strategies

- Don't think of stopping as an exercise, but rather a pop quiz. If your horse won't stand still, like the horse in Photo 6A, don't attempt to force him to stand; that can result in a fight you lose. Instead, return to Step 1 and work through the exercise slowly, advancing only as your horse is ready. Work on precision, increasing the repetitions and expecting more from your horse each time. Soon he figures out that the extra work is harder than complying with your cues the first time.

- Your horse might turn to look at his buddy. If he does, use direct-rein pressure to direct your horse's head where you want it.

- If you don't have a trail partner, but do have the confidence and competence, you still can break your horse's buddy-bound behavior. Go to a riding area with enough trails to physically challenge your horse. It's important that you know the trails and that the trails offer you options to lengthen or shorten the ride. Just a mile of trail work at a trot might challenge a 2-year-old, while a 3-year-old might be challenged by two miles, and an older horse might need five to 10 miles to be challenged. Make sure someone reliable knows your route and schedule.

  Push your horse onto the trail at a trot. Perform serpentines and other maneuvers to capture his attention, as in Photo 6B. When the horse gets distracted, ask him to trot a little faster. Keep him too busy to get out of control. At each descent, ask him to collect. On level ground, ask him to move to one side of the trail, and then the other. As your horse relaxes, you also will relax and start asking him to do something. By the time the horse finally says, "Okay, boss, you have my attention. What are we doing?" you should be on the way back to your trailer at a walk. With patience, repetition and consistency, your mount develops independence and can be ridden anywhere you want to go—alone.

KINSEY'S KEYS TO SUCCESS

- **Work in a controlled environment.** Control is key in this lesson, as with anything you do with your horse. Start this exercise in a familiar environment, where your horse is relaxed, obedient and can focus on you without many distractions.

- **Don't get forced into a fight.** Don't try to force control, or you might cause a confrontation that no one wins. Keep your horse working to avoid his taking control. You and I can't make the horse do anything, but we can keep him working until he realizes he can't do whatever he wants. When your horse doesn't get his way, he associates extra work with his failure to listen, and being rewarded with less work when he does listen. Then you get cooperation.

- **Get him in the right mindset.** Before you venture where your horse can test or take advantage of you, ride him in a round pen, longe him or ground-drive him. (See Chapter 7, "Ground-Driving.") This takes off the edge and gets him attuned to you. Don't attempt to ride until he consistently obeys. As a guideline, work him for at least 10 to 15 minutes, but it's better to work for success, rather than a particular amount of time.

- **Think light.** Find the point where you make just enough rein contact with your horse that you remain in control yet aren't in his mouth. If you make too much contact, he might get excited, and possibly angry. Too little, and he might ignore you.

- **Practice patience.** Training your horse takes time, patience and repetition, so plan plenty of time on your trail rides to practice this lesson. Depending on your horse's training and disposition, practicing an exercise once might do the trick, or he might require several repetitions and practice sessions to develop confidence.

- **Cue consistently.** In order for your horse to understand your cues and consistently deliver the same response, you must cue him exactly the same way each time.

- **Stay relaxed.** If you remain cool and confident, even if your horse panics, you offer assurance, and he soon follows your lead.

- **Keep a safe distance.** When riding single file, allow plenty of distance between horses to avoid getting kicked. The rear rider should be able to see the front horse's heels between the rear horse's ears.

- **Build on success.** After your ride, talk with your riding partner about what went well and what needs improvement. When you recognize your strengths and weaknesses and solicit feedback from experienced riders, you continue to improve.

- **Use common sense.** Finally, if you feel as though you and your horse are in danger, stop and seek help from a knowledgeable horseman.

Prevent your horse from trying to sneak a snack on the trail with this no-force technique.

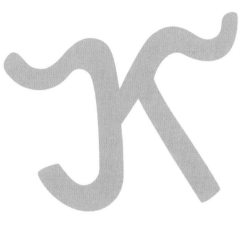

15

SNACK ATTACK

When you ride down the trail, does your horse dive for bites of grass every chance he gets, jerking your arms and pulling you forward? If so, you probably tug continually on the reins and his mouth to keep his head up. This can frustrate both you and your horse or desensitize your horse, causing other problems, such as a lack of response or resistance to the bit. Also, your horse risks stepping on his reins or getting a foot caught. The harsh, sudden pull on the bit might frighten him or cause him to jerk up his head, rear or stumble. Any of these situations could mean your trail ride ends in an unplanned trip to the emergency room.

In this chapter, I explain why your horse has the urge to munch along the trailside, how to prevent snacking behavior and how to control the annoying habit if your horse already has developed it.

Before you perform this lesson, your horse must have the following skills:

- Move forward, backward and stop willingly.

- Yield laterally to leg and direct-rein pressure in both directions.

- Readily perform circles, straight lines and serpentines at all gaits.

Snacking Source

Get to the root of your horse's snacking behavior to help prevent the problem. Horses are natural grazers. When they see tall, lush grass, they instinctively want to plunge for a bite. If you don't pay attention to your

NECESSARY EQUIPMENT

- **Bridle with smooth-mouthed snaffle bit, chin strap (bit hobble) and split reins.** A snaffle bit lack shanks, giving you direct contact with the corners of your horse's mouth when you ride two-handed. This makes it easier for you to control his head and encourage him to soften and perform the exercise. A chin strap simply prevents you from pulling the bit through your horse's mouth.

- **Saddle and blanket (or pad).**

horse or ride actively, you invite him to eat, thereby redirecting his focus from you to the grass. If you daydream in the saddle, your horse might also munch on branches and vines that he normally would not. In essence, your inattentiveness, not your horse, is the problem. A horse that has been gently, but firmly, corrected for snacking won't challenge his rider for the snack. Snacking is learned behavior.

The key to stopping your horse's trailside snacking: Become the driver, not the passenger. Anticipate your horse's moves and direct his attention onto you rather than the grass, before he goes for a bite. Your horse might be preparing to plunge his head into the grass when he slows down, tugs on the reins and starts to lower his head. An experienced snacker might dart his head out for a bite to prevent you from having time to stop him.

Prevention

1. Monitor your horse and surroundings. To prevent your horse from developing this annoying habit, watch for snacking signs. Look ahead for possible grazing opportunities, so you can redirect your horse's attention, as Lauren does in Photo 1, before the problem arises

2. Keep him busy. To occupy your horse's mind, give him familiar requests, followed by corrections. For example, apply left leg pressure to move him to the right side of the trail. Then reward him by releasing the pressure and walking straight a couple of steps. Then reverse your cues and repeat toward the other side of the trail, rewarding after each repetition. Another option: Tip your horse's nose 1 inch to the left and release the pressure to walk straight when he com-

plies, as as shown in Photo 2 on the next page. Then ask him to tip his nose 2 inches to the right and so forth, releasing after each attempt. It doesn't matter what you request, as long as you clearly request it, correct your horse and reward him with release. Request frequency depends on his attentiveness to you, his history of being allowed to mentally wander and his determination to get his way.

3. Cure the munchies. Pay attention to your horse. A horse usually slows and lowers his head before snacking; both signal he's about to grab a bite of grass. Watch for these signs in your horse, and be ready to take action. If your horse dives for a bite, or acts as though he might, avoid pulling his head straight up with reins—a common reaction with amateurs. That only sets you up for a tug of war that your horse eventually wins. He might also rear and develop other vices, such as

fighting or ignoring the bit. Instead, teach your horse to associate snacking behavior with work. Stay calm, immediately and briskly pick up on one rein, and use direct-rein pressure to demand he raise his head and turn, as shown in Photo 3 above. Simultaneously use your seat, leg and voice cues to drive him forward at a trot. If necessary, pop his hip with the rein ends to drive him forward. At the trot, things happen fast enough for you to get his attention and make it difficult for a determined muncher to grab that bite. With repetition and your consistency, he learns that bite of grass isn't worth the extra effort.

Problem-Solving Strategies

• Monitor your horse's reaction to your correction. If you undercorrect or correct too slowly, you merely encourage him to become sly about darting out his head to grab a bite. If you overcorrect, your horse might panic or become confused.

Each horse requires different levels of correction. Watch your horse to adjust and fine-tune your correction to get the desired response.

• If your horse lugs on your rein and/or sticks out his nose to counter your direct-rein guidance, firmly bump the direct rein in the direction you want his face to go, and demand he trot. If necessary, bump the rein a second or third time. Intensify your consistent guidance, telling your horse you mean "turn." If you allow your horse to rebel, you create a dangerous horse, just as if you allow him to bite or kick without appropriate discipline he understands.

• If your horse attempts to buck, pin his ears, move against your cues or perform any other willful action, firmly correct him. More importantly, recognize that the display is based on disrespect for you and

your guidance. If you can't correct this potentially dangerous attitude immediately, use daily round-pen work to get your horse's attention and respect before you ride. Some spoiled horses, those considered by their owners as "pets," need round-pen warm-ups every day of their lives.

4. Perform a training maneuver. Once your horse trots, ask him to perform familiar training maneuvers, such as flexing, circling or weaving along the trail. Practice bending and turning him at a trot until you have his full attention. Ride two-handed so you can easily and effectively direct him. The key: Keep your horse moving and listening to you, so he doesn't think about sneaking a bite. He soon learns that reaching for that snack means extra work.

Problem-Solving Strategies
- If your horse pulls on the reins or sticks out his nose, firmly tug or bump the direct rein until you have his attention.

- If your horse even thinks about eating, urge him forward, still at a trot, and make him work harder, so it's nearly impossible for him to grab a bite of grass. When he obeys your directional cues, indicating you have his attention, slow to a walk.

- Avoid loping. At this gait, too many things happen too quickly, and you increase the risk of falling off. A walk might be too slow to gain and maintain your horse's attention.

5. Continue training. Incorporate directional changes into your maneuvers, reinforcing your focus-on-me message. Ride in this manner until your horse willingly responds to your requests. Then slow to a walk and test your horse's dependability. If he goes for the grass, repeat Steps 1 and 2, until he's no longer distracted by his belly. If you pay close attention to your horse's actions and work him through this lesson when eating becomes an issue, you quickly overcome his snack attacks.

Problem-Solving Strategies

- If your horse becomes bored and shifts his attention to the grass, ask him to perform more arduous maneuvers, such as stops, backs and rollbacks, trotting between maneuvers, as shown in Photos 5A and 5B.

KINSEY'S KEYS TO SUCCESS

- **Remain attentive so your horse is alert.** Keeping your horse focused on what you want is key. Eating, spooking, rubbing against trees, stumbling and a host of other problems can be prevented, or at least mitigated, by keeping your horse attuned to your requests. When your horse is fresh, make requests every 5 to 10 steps to keep his attention.

- **Adjust your attitude.** Think of this correction as a positive training opportunity, rather than a nuisance. You must have the right attitude to get your horse in the right mindset.

- **Don't be a passenger.** If you allow your horse to be the driver, you allow him to take control, putting you in a dangerous situation.

- **Anticipate.** Look ahead for areas where your horse might try to eat, such as a lush meadow, so you can prepare to take charge before he attempts to nibble. Adjust your rein length to the point you have maximum control without pulling on his mouth. Don't wait until the issue arises to adjust your rein length, or you delay your guidance, allowing him to take control. Your goal is to keep him busy with training maneuvers to prevent him from going for the grass.

- **Pick your battles.** If you pull on your horse's mouth with two reins, you only initiate a fight you eventually lose. Instead, use clear, consistent direct-rein cues to turn him and get him back on track, focused on you.

- **Start 'em right!** An ounce of correction when an issue first comes up is worth more than a lifetime of nagging misery. It's much easier to keep your horse focused and under control if you never allow him to develop bad habits, e.g. eating while being ridden, bucking, bolting, shaking, rubbing against trees, lying down in the river, etc.

Teach your chargey horse that being at the back of the pack isn't so bad with these patience-building exercises.

16

THE NEED TO LEAD

Whenever you start on a group trail ride, unless he's the lead animal, your horse revs his motor, as though he's at the starting line for a race. He focuses ahead, chomps on the bit, jerks the reins, tosses his head, jigs and bucks. Paying no attention to you or the other horses in front of him, he shoves his way into the lead. Once in front, he relaxes, slows down and behaves decently.

Sound familiar? If your horse must be the boss on the trail, you need to take control of him now—before someone gets hurt. There are too many chargey horses for all to be in the lead. Besides being irritating, a chargey horse is a hazard to you and everyone around him. Until he gets his way, he rides too closely behind other horses, putting you at risk for getting kicked. He also pushes into a group of horses, creating a compromising situation and crowding other riders off the trail.

In this chapter, I get to the root of your horse's need to lead, and explain how to take control of him and teach him to ride where you dictate within the group.

Before you begin, work your horse in a round pen and practice the ground-driving exercise outline in Chapter 7, "Ground-Driving." Then gradually advance to riding your horse in the round pen, and eventually working him in open areas, so you don't jeopardize other riders while training your horse. Also, your horse must proficiently perform the following skills:

- Move forward, move backward and stop readily.

- Yield laterally to direct-rein pressure in both directions.

Note: If you ride a stallion, he requires special handling. For your safety and that of others on the trail, seek help from a professional, and consider gelding him if he isn't used for breeding.

Follow the Leader

There are three primary underlying reasons for your horse's fight-to-the-front behavior. The leading causes involve his rank in the herd hierarchy and fear of being left behind and ambushed by a predator. As I've discussed in previous chapters, horses, as herd animals, depend on their herd mates for survival. If a predator threatens, the herd relies on the lead horse to direct it to safety. When you trail ride, you change the herd organization, thus taking your horse out of his comfort zone.

For example, you try to control your horse's position in line, and you direct him where you want to go. If your horse is used to being the leader, he's likely to become insecure toward the back, where he's a prime target for predators. Or, if he's not used to leading, he also becomes nervous because there's not another horse to guide him.

A secondary cause: You're unaware of your responsibility as a rider and inadvertently train the horse to act this way by what you do or don't do. For example, if you frequently race against riding buddies or drill your horse on timed events, you encourage

him to charge. You need to establish a balanced riding program that includes sufficient controlled, relaxed riding. A general rule: For every timed ride, include five to 10 relaxing, controlled rides.

Another example: If you allow your horse to bounce around when he's excited, afraid or angry, you inadvertently develop a chargey horse. Instead, to control your horse's nervous energy, put him to work with the techniques in this exercise.

In this chapter, we approach the problem as a training correction, rather than a disciplinary issue, because no matter the reason, the problem is still instinctual.

Developing a trusting relationship with your horse and focusing his attention on you helps resolve his rush. However, this takes patience and perseverance. Avoid punishment, as it only escalates the bad (instinctual) behavior. Instead, patiently and gradually train your horse, regarding the slightest effort as a step toward achieving a bond based on trust and confidence. Don't fall into panic mode, attempting to insist your horse stop or stand still. It's not going to happen. You lose control of your horse, and the harder you try to contain that nervous energy, the more of an explosion you encounter. Control that nervous energy by diffusing it through work.

Simple Solution

1. Start at the back. Begin toward the back of the group, riding two-handed with direct-rein control and remaining relaxed. If your horse gets excited and tries to surge ahead, don't punish or fight him; you only exacerbate the problem. Also, avoid tensing and pulling back on the reins, or your horse could rear. Instead, go to Step 2.

2. Turn your horse. Once your horse tries to forge forward, ignoring your soft two-rein request to slow and maintain his distance from the horse in front, cue your horse to turn around. Most likely he ignores your cue. Immediately, with one rein loose, use the direct rein to haul the horse into a tight circle. As the horse completes 360 degrees, release the horse and allow him to follow the horse ahead. Leave both reins loose, relax, breath and smile. You have begun to teach control.

As your horse closes on the leading horse again, with two reins ask your horse to slow down softly. If your horse doesn't slow, cue him to turn around in the opposite direction.

If he doesn't respond adequately to the cue, with one rein loose, use the direct rein to guide him into a tight circle. As your horse completes the 360 degrees, release the direct rein, breath, relax and smile. You're no longer fighting your horse, you're getting into his head. Continue until you notice some improvement, and watch for the trail to widen.

3. Ride to the front. Find a wide spot in the trail and jog ahead of the group to the point your horse can't see the rest of the herd. This puts his nervous energy to work and pushes him through his comfort zone to where he feels insecure and, thus, learns to listen to you. At that point, start to gain control of the situation. When your trail mates are out of sight, your horse might become nervous. That's okay; just like any other training lesson, whenever he misbehaves, you must make him uncomfortable to get him focused on you and encourage the desired behavior. Simply put him to work, as described in Step 2.

Problem-Solving Strategies

• Be sure to let the group know your plans, so they can move their horses to the edge of the trail to provide plenty of passing room. Discuss the issue, the training plan, and options before mounting up. In the heat of the issue is not a time conducive to discussion.

- If your horse remains out of control at the front of the group, it's a sign he's not confident in his surroundings or has too much energy. Chances are you don't have the control necessary to ride on a wide-open trail. To establish control, return to the round pen and practice the ground-driving exercise outlined in Chapter 7. Then gradually advance to ride your horse in the pen and eventually in the open.

- Ride with people who are interested in safety and understand riding to the level of the person who has the most difficulty.

- The most frantic behavior from a horse comes when the group speeds off and leaves the horse. The easiest way to grab the horse's mind, if you are a competent and confident rider, is to push the horse away from the group first, letting the group know where you'll link up with them. "I'm going up the trail for a mile, be back in 10 minutes," or "Meet you at the river crossing."

4. Perform familiar maneuvers. Once your horse is in the lead, perform simple maneuvers to encourage him to relax and listen to you. For example, practice serpentines, as shown, or walk-jog-walk transitions. To keep him driving forward, gently squeeze your legs against his sides and lean your torso forward slightly. When he complies with your cues, allow him to take a few free steps, then repeat. Continue working your horse your horse until he forgets about the group and takes his cues from you.

Problem-Solving Strategies

- Expect your horse to fret; you've taken him beyond his comfort zone. Be confident, firm, and keep him busy. Just like a teenager, when your horse is busy, he has less time to get into trouble.

- If you're not confident in your skills and ability to stay cool and in control, enlist the help of a friend with confidence, a cool head and firm hands the first few rides. Or, consider professional training to jump-start you and the horse on the trail to success.

- Don't count on neck-reining or other subtle cues to work on a stressed horse.

5

NECESSARY EQUIPMENT

- **Bridle with a smooth-mouthed snaffle bit, chin strap (bit hobble) and split reins.** All of these allow you to ride two-handed and apply direct-rein pressure for added control and crystal-clear cues. Secure a chin strap to the rings to prevent pulling the bit through your horse's mouth. Adjust the strap so you can fit only two fingers between the strap and your horse's chin.

- **Saddle and blanket or pad.** Avoid excessively thick pads that could cause equine discomfort and saddle slippage. You don't want to misinterpret your horse's pain for disobedience.

- **Experienced riding partner(s) with quiet, obedient horse(s).** It's best to work among a small group of understanding riding buddies, rather than on a public ride; riding ahead of the trail boss might be frowned upon or your training could disrupt the ride. All riders need to understand that safety and training are priority. In case you inadvertently get in a sticky situation, make sure the horses aren't apt to kick.

- **Suitable trail.** Always select a trail that complements your and your horse's abilities. For this problem-solving exercise or green horses and riders, a gradual, rolling, wide trail with solid footing is best.

Use defensive-riding techniques with direct-rein cues and correct the horse until he listens to you.

5. Ride circles. Next, walk your horse in large circles, moving toward and then away from the group to gauge his responsiveness and prepare him to re-enter the pack quietly, as in Photo 5. To circle to the right, use your right rein to direct your horse's nose around the turn. Simultaneously release your right leg to give him freedom to turn. Support him around the circle with your left leg and left neck-rein cue.

Problem-Solving Strategies
- If your horse becomes out of control on the way back to the group, ride away again, as outlined in Step 2. To bust his bossy behavior, you might need to repeat this technique on several rides.

- If you have a high-energy horse, or one that repeatedly has been allowed to have his way, you might want to push him at a trot for 30 minutes or longer, depending on his conditioning. Plan to meet your group back at the trailer or at a shady intersection. As you wait, tie your horse to a solid post or hobble him, if he's accustomed to hobbles, to practice patience until the group arrives. Repeat as necessary.

6. Halt. When your horse willingly and quietly circles toward the group, test his patience and focus by halting until the group catches up. Keep him moving until you feel he's ready to stop. You'll know he's ready when his energy decreases, he slows his feet and isn't adamant

about accelerating out of a turn. Then ride a few more minutes so that when you ask him to stop, it's a reward. At first, don't expect your horse to stand still. Simply drive him forward if he becomes fidgety. Continue riding until he focuses on you, is free of nervous energy, accepts you as the "lead" horse, and complies with your cues and directives. When you consistently use stopping as a reward for hard work, you end up with a trail horse others will envy.

Problem-Solving Strategies
- If your horse shifts his focus onto his trail buddies or wants to charge ahead, avoid pulling back on the reins, or you induce more excitement and a potential rear. Learn to think ahead so you don't directly fight the horse. Instead, keep him busy with the circling maneuver outlined in Step 5. Continue this exercise, ahead of the group, until he's focused on you. Then ask him to stand still again. If he does, you've achieved your goal. If not, send him back to work.

7. Circle into or behind the group. When your horse willingly circles in front of the group, and stands still and waits for them, increase the exercise's difficulty. Further test his behavior by gradually circling him through or behind the group, using the technique outlined in Step 5.

When you find a comfortable spot in the group, take your horse's mind off the lead position by weaving on the trail, practicing speed transitions and halting, if possible. Be sure to keep your riding buddies informed of your activities, so they can maintain a

171

safe distance. When your horse is comfortable and listening to you, gradually circle farther back.

As your horse becomes attentive to you, he starts to quietly walk anywhere in the group you choose. When that happens, your trail rides become more relaxing and enjoyable for you and your horse. To maintain that pleasant attitude, routinely change your horse's riding position within the group. Remember: If you continue to the front of the line, make sure it's your decision, not your horse's.

Problem-Solving Strategies

• Should your horse become restless, he's shifted his focus back on the group, rather than you. Simply send him back to work again. This time, gradually circle farther back into the group as he gains confidence.

Note: You might need to ride out of sight again. Depending on your horse's breeding, disposition and past success at misbehaving, he might require several repetitions to learn that his nervous, silly behavior doesn't allow him to move where he wants.

KINSEY'S KEYS TO SUCCESS

- **Work in a controlled environment.** Control is essential for anything you do with your horse. Start in a familiar environment, where your horse is relaxed, obedient and can focus on you without many distractions.

- **Work out the fresh.** Before you venture out, ride your horse in a round pen, longe or ground-drive him. This takes off the edge and gets him listening to you. Rather than working him for a set amount of time, train until he consistently obeys.

- **Take a light feel.** To teach your horse to ride on a loose rein, you need to be willing to ride on a loose rein, and apply corrections as required. If you maintain rein contact with your horse all the time, he never gets that soft "yes boss?" listening response that we all want. If you "nag" with too much contact, your horse learns to ignore you, or he might get excited and possibly angry. Use a light, gentle cue to which you think he'll respond, then correct him as necessary. If you consistently do this, you and your horse begin to communicate in quiet, subtle cues that you'll both appreciate.

- **Be patient.** Training your horse takes time, patience and repetition, so plan plenty of time on your trail rides to practice the lesson. Depending on your horse's training and disposition, practicing these exercises once might do the trick, or he might require several repetitions and practice sessions to develop confidence. Be ready to spend as much time as necessary on a training session or to ride until you see improvement. Quitting during misbehavior rewards misbehavior and nets more misbehavior. Quitting when things are improving rewards the improvement and yields better behavior.

- **Avoid one-rein stops that become rest breaks.** These rest breaks are rewards immediately at the end of poor behavior. Rewarding poor behavior results in more poor behavior.

- **Avoid overflexing that brings the horse's nose to the rider's leg.** While doing that might get some temporary control, two undesirable side effects can occur. First, a frustrated horse may inflict a severe bite on the rider's leg. Worse, a horse that is exposed to overflexing can learn to "rubberneck," or move in a lateral direction away from his head. This is undesirable in a show ring, and absolutely dangerous in a trail horse. Think about it—having a horse bent and focused on your left leg while he moves laterally to his right. The horse is unable to see where he is going. Falling over logs, embankments or into dangerous obstacles can result.

- **Communicate consistently.** In order for your horse to understand your cues and consistently deliver the same response, you must cue him exactly the same way each time.

- **Keep your cool.** If you remain cool and confident, even if your horse panics initially, he soon follows your lead.

- **Remain at a safe distance.** To avoid getting kicked, allow plenty of distance between horses. You should be able to see the heels of the horse in front of you between your horse's ears.

- **Build on success.** To build his confidence and confirm the correct response, reward your horse for the slightest effort. The smallest steps lay a strong foundation of trust and obedience.

- **Use common sense.** Finally, if you feel as though you and your horse are in danger, stop and seek help from a knowledgeable horseman.

Overcome your horse's kicking behavior with this correction-and-prevention process.

17

KICK CONTROL

If you've ever been on an organized trail ride, you're probably aware of the red-flag rule: Don't approach a horse with a red flag in its tail from behind or you'll likely get kicked. Although I think this is a good safety measure, especially while you're correcting the problem, I don't think it should be an excuse for not gaining control of your horse.

Kicking horses are not only difficult to handle on the ground and under saddle, but they're also downright dangerous. Although it's best to eliminate this problem before it becomes a habit, that's not always an option, especially if your horse already was handy with his hindquarters when you got him.

To help you break this dangerous pattern, I explain why your horse lashes out with his hindquarters. Then I tell you how to recognize that a kick is imminent and outline my correction-and-prevention program. Kicking is one of the easiest problems to prevent; yet the remedy is one of the hardest to teach.

To successfully apply my kick-control program, first make sure your horse has the following prerequisites:

- Stands quietly and tolerates being sacked out.

- Moves forward, backward and stops readily upon your request.

- Yields laterally to direct-rein pressure in both directions.

- Reacts positively to being corrected.

Kicking Causes

As with most of the behavioral issues covered in this trail-training book, fear, herd-ranking and/or lack of respect are at the core of your horse's heels-up reaction. Kicking under saddle or on a lead line is the result of inadequate training. For some horses, kicking is a means of fending off predators. If another horse, human or dog suddenly approaches your horse from behind, there's a good

chance your horse can't see the "attacker," thinks "predator" and kicks in self-defense. Your horse also might kick to establish his role as herd leader or, in this case, trail boss.

Some folks who ride mares blame kicking behavior on the mares' heat cycles. I don't tolerate moodiness, and you shouldn't either. As for stallions, riding a stallion or with someone who does is inherently dangerous and outside the scope of this article. If a rider can't handle kicking, that rider probably isn't experienced enough to handle a stallion. I can't emphasize how much those ignorant of the potential and possibly deadly consequences of kicking too often ride stallions around other horses. It's better to just say "No" to a riding partner than suffer the consequences.

In all cases, the key to controlling a kicking horse lies in your ability to communicate with the horse and your ability to keep your horse listening to you. You must first recognize signs that a kick is imminent and comprehend his motivation before you can make an appropriate correction.

Kicking out of fear and insecurity requires correction and training, while aggression and dominance need correction and discipline. Focus your horse's attention on something else, such as a training maneuver. This establishes your authority and, in time, helps overcome the horse's insecurity or aggressiveness, and develops his trust in your control. Then you can remove the red ribbons forever.

Simple Solution

1. Recognize the signs. Learn to read your horse's body language, so you know when kicking is on his mind, and you can adjust his attitude before he elevates his feet. Surefire signs of kicking include a raised head, pinned ears, swishing tail and slightly turned head to get a clear rear view, as the Paint demonstrates in Photo 1. Your horse also might slow and tense. If you notice these signs, a kick soon could follow. Even if you don't ride a "kicker" yet, follow these steps to prevent your horse from learning to kick.

2. Redirect his attention. If you spot the signs, immediately and aggressively direct your horse's attention off his kicking target and onto you, before he has a chance to raise his heels. Circle him away from the intended target or drive him forward. To circle him,

2

NECESSARY EQUIPMENT

- **Bridle with a smooth-mouthed snaffle bit, chin strap (bit hobble) and split reins.** Split reins and a snaffle give you the direct-rein control you need to guide your horse, while a properly adjusted chin strap prevents pulling the bit through the horse's mouth.

  I ride with 7- or 8-foot, heavy harness-leather reins. If my horse attempts to kick, I pop his rump with the rein ends. If you're not proficient with using the reins in this manner, use a crop or whip (see below). Flopping reins are counterproductive. If you miss the horse's rump and pop your back, you could become distracted at an inconvenient time.

- **Saddle and blanket (or pad).**

- **Riding crop or whip.** Most riding crops are about 25 inches long with a 2-inch, broad leather popper, while whips are longer with a long, narrow popper or lash.

  If the horse kicks due to fear or insecurity, use a riding crop to pop his rump. This provides enough additional motivation to follow your guidance without inducing fear. Until you're comfortable using a crop, secure a wrist strap to the handle and slip it over your wrist, allowing the crop to dangle. When you need the crop, simply swing your arm back with your hand open. The handle automatically slips into your hand without you having to reach for it.

On the other hand, if the horse kicks because he's established dominance, use a riding whip to correct him. The slight sting and stronger discipline isn't abusive, but help you gain his attention quickly and easily.

- **Experienced riding partner(s) with quiet, obedient horse(s).** For safety and consideration, it's best to correct your horse's kicking behavior among supportive riding buddies, rather than a group of strangers on a paid, public ride.

- **Wide trail.** You ask your horse to circle and perform maneuvers for this correction, so it's best to work on a wide, flat or moderately sloped trail with solid footing, where you can focus on your horse, not the terrain. A narrow trail does not mean you can't perform these maneuvers, it just means you must be prepared to demonstrate additional control, confidence and competence.

- **Safety gear.** Your riding partners might consider donning chaps or knee and shin guards to help protect their legs in case they misjudge your horse, or you fail to deter his kicking. It's a good idea for all riders to wear helmets when working around horses with behavioral issues. Although it's not reflected in these photos, we wear helmets when working with any problem horses.

---

use your inside rein to direct his nose in the direction you want.

For example, to circle to the left, as shown in Photo 2, use your left rein to tip his nose in that direction. At the same time, move your inside leg away from your horse's side to "open the gate" to movement in that direction, and support him through the turn with outside neck-rein and leg pressure.

To drive him forward, slightly tip your pelvis forward, loosen your reins and squeeze his sides with your calves. Reinforce your cues with verbal commands as necessary. However, keep in mind that constantly harassing your horse verbally does not do any good and might irritate your friends.

Problem-Solving Strategies
- If your horse kicks or fails to move immediately at your request, pop his rump with the riding whip. He must learn that you expect immediate and full cooperation.

- Don't merely tap your horse with the whip, or he could learn to associate the tap as a cue or even become desensitized to the

whip. You want him to recognize that the whip means he reacted too slowly to your cues.

- Don't allow your feet to slide back along the horse's sides. If he kicks, you must be able to slide your feet ahead of your hips and shoulders to brace while, at the same time, you turn him around and drive him forward with your legs and/or whip. Failure to place your feet out in front might result in being thrust forward or off your horse if he kicks. Failure to take action to control the horse means that you encourage the misbehavior.

3. Keep him busy. Next, ask your horse to perform familiar requests, such as the circles, serpentines or flexing maneuvers as previously outlined and shown in Photo 3. Doing so occupies his mind and legs, and focuses his attention on you, so he forgets about kicking.

Whatever activity you choose, make sure your cues are clear. Correct your horse as necessary to prevent other problems and

KINSEY'S KEYS TO SUCCESS

- **Be observant.** The critical key is to anticipate situations that might induce a kick, to interrupt your horse's intention to kick and to transition into getting your horse busy with work. With an association of intense work every time he thinks of kicking, the kicking becomes an event he wants to avoid.

- **Stay away from spurs and curb bits.** Used incorrectly, both can do more harm than good. Persistent jabbing or jerking could trigger your horse to kick, buck, bolt or rear, not what you hope to accomplish. Furthermore, there is a tendency to "grab" with one's legs or hands when startled or panicked. Grabbing with your legs and spurs or with your hands and the bit surprises and might even annoy or panic your horse to the point of beginning a rodeo you could do without. If you horse works off spur cues or is accustomed to spur corrections, spurs might be appropriate. However, spurs and curb bits are used most appropriately by experienced trainers on well-broke horses, not recreational riders trying to fix problems.

- **Train for success.** Building your horse's confidence and reprogramming his behavior takes much time, as well as persistence. Expecting quick results or using force and intimidation to achieve these goals spoils your chances for long-term success.

- **Cue consistently.** Continue to use the same cues you've used throughout this training series so your instructions are apparent to your horse, further increasing his responsiveness.

- **Keep your distance.** A key to avoiding and overcoming kicking is to allow plenty of distance between horses in your group. See Photo 4B and the text below for specific spacing guidelines for safety.

reward him with release or a break when he's attentive to you.

Repeat Steps 1 through 3 anytime your horse shows signs of kicking. In time, he discovers that you call the shots on the trail and that kicking isn't worth the extra effort.

Problem-Solving Strategies

- Firmly correct and/or discipline your horse. Otherwise, he learns to cheat or hides his intentions before he kicks (or bites)—an extremely dangerous situation. Rather than changing his ideas on what's right, he simply changes his ideas on getting caught. When that happens, you have no choice but to live with the consequences. Spare your horse and yourself the risk by being assertive now, before your horse's behavior escalates.

- Create adequate space between horses. Can you point out the major safety violation in Photo 4A? There isn't enough distance between horses. Just as people don't like to have their personal space invaded, horses feel threatened when a "predator" or another horse gets dangerously close.

- As a general rule, to help prevent the temptation to kick, keep at least a horse-length between riders, as shown in Photo 4B. The rear rider should be able to see, between his horse's ears, the leading horse's heels.

- If your horse crowds too closely on the heels of another horse, you have the perfect opportunity to work on collecting or shifting your horse's weight onto his hind quarters, or to practice a turnaround, as in Photo 4C. When turning, communicate with other riders and safely merge back into line to prevent another jam. If things are a bit tight, call out "Turning!" so the riders behind can either slow, stop, or turn, as well. I make sure my riders know this is a part of training, an opportunity to excel, and not a reason to be irritated.

Mind your manners on multiuse trails with these rules of conduct.

18

TRAIL ETIQUETTE

In the past, hikers and hunters were the only other humans horseback riders encountered in the backcountry. Today, however, more people seek respite from the city, thus are pursuing various forms of outdoor recreation from dirt biking to rock climbing. Although some areas have equestrian-only trails, most areas require that hikers, bikers, horseback riders and other outdoor enthusiasts share the same paths. Unfortunately, conflict among user groups has limited access to public lands. To ensure that future horsemen have open spaces to ride, you must become a trail-riding ambassador, respecting other users, following trail rules and leaving only hoof prints.

Here, I offer trail-etiquette tips to help you coexist with other trail riders and users and leave positive impressions. The most important things to remember on the trail are to use common sense and to have fun!

Park your trailer straight and efficiently so you, as well as other riders and vehicles, can maneuver safely through the parking area and without blocking access.

Leave the parking area as clean as or cleaner than you found it, which also means disposing of all manure.

At the Trail Head

Your responsibilities as a trail rider start long before you step into the saddle. Here are some guidelines to follow at the trail head.

- **Arrive early.** On scheduled group rides, arrive at the trail head ahead of schedule. That way you have time to gather and inspect your gear, saddle and work your horse, and still be ready to ride on time.

- **Park efficiently.** Consider other riders when parking your rig. Allow plenty of room between trailers, so other riders and horses tied to trailers aren't at risk of getting kicked. Also, make sure your trailer doesn't block another rig. Some folks don't

know how to back their trailers properly. In order to pull out easily, they sometimes take up a lot of parking space that could be used by other riders. Too often folks park for their convenience, rather than considering the normal parking pattern.

- **Clean up.** Dispose of all trash in garbage cans. Scoop manure into a pile to be removed, or spread it away from picnic areas, so it becomes natural fertilizer.

Riding in Groups

Riding with friends and family is fun, but keep in mind the guidelines outlined below for safety and courtesy. Before leaving the trail head, discuss the upcoming ride, issues, problem areas, hand signals or other control measures and the following rules. Understanding the group rules promotes safety and fun for all.

- **Wait for the group.** On group trail rides, ride off only when all riders are ready and mounted. Otherwise, the horse left behind might become difficult to mount or run to catch up with the rest of the group. The same rule applies at gates and other obstacles where a rider might dismount.

- **Stay behind the trail boss.** The lead rider is in charge of guiding the group safely along the trail and sticking to a set schedule. He can't efficiently do his job if group members ride ahead.

- **Separate unfriendly horses.** If two horses don't get along, space them far apart in the line. This helps prevent a wreck, plus makes the ride more enjoyable for everyone.

- **Announce gait changes.** The leader should travel at a pace that's comfortable for all horses in the group and is suited to the abilities of the least experienced horse and rider. To prevent surprises and potential accidents, announce gait changes well in advance so your companions are prepared. Also, wait to jog or lope until the rear riders clear obstacles and arrive at a level, suitable spot to increase the pace. Picking up the pace unannounced or while riders are negotiating obstacles is inconsiderate, dangerous and could cause some horses to panic and try to catch up to the

Designate a leader on your rides, and stay behind that person so he or she can guide you safely.

Develop hand signals everyone in the group understands so the trail boss can communicate interesting sights to see or potential problems.

Separate unfamiliar or unfriendly horses to prevent wrecks.

herd. To signal the group to stop, hold up your hand. For large groups or on winding trails, slow down gradually to avoid a pileup.

- **Point out hazards.** The leader should notify other riders of upcoming hazards, such as low branches and water crossings, and make sure everyone in the group crosses safely before moving too far ahead. Simply pointing out potential danger zones could save the cost of a veterinary or doctor bill. Use a different hand signal to point out areas of interest versus potential pitfalls. A hand signal is understood more clearly at a distance than are attempts to verbalize. In my program, pointing toward an object with the index finger with the thumb pointing down signals danger, horses picketed off the trail or any other thing that might surprise horse and rider.

- **Don't drink and ride.** Just as drinking alcoholic beverages impairs your driving ability, it also mars your control and common sense while horseback. Most horsemen recognize that riding well and assisting a horse through obstacles requires attention and focus. Your horse deserves your best, but drinking before or while riding exposes him to your worst.

- **Maintain adequate distance.** To help avoid getting kicked, allow at least one horse length between your horse and the rider in front of you. Ideally, you should see the heels of the horse in front of you between your horse's ears. Even a well-trained horse has the potential to kick when threatened. A horse following too closely focuses on the lead horse, rather than his rider's directions. Therefore, if the lead horse spooks, the "tail-focused" horse likely spooks, too.

- **Control your horse.** You're responsible for your horse's behavior. If you've practiced the techniques outlined in previous chapters, you have the skills necessary to control your horse on the trail, whether he kicks, jigs, spooks at obstacles, rushes to the front of the group or lags behind. Being able to correct these problems reduces the risk of danger to you, your horse and other trail users. About the only behavioral issue I haven't covered is nipping. If your horse

Don't get caught trailing this close. Maintain about a horse's length between you and the rider in front.

tries to nip at another horse, use direct-rein pressure to turn his head away from the other horse as you drive your horse forward. If you don't achieve success, slap his rump with the ends of your reins to reinforce the punishment. Your horse's level of training isn't fixed, so positively influence it. Your horse either does what you *allow* him to do, or what you *direct* him to do.

- **Keep slow horses in the rear.** A horse that must trot part of the time to keep up is a real nuisance. The repetitive trot-walk transitions are distracting to other horses and their riders.

- **Prevent the accordion effect.** Make sure the entire group understands the accordion effect—people becoming bunched up or overly spread out—and rides to counteract it. To clarify the accordion effect, imagine riders maneuvering up and down hilly terrain. The leaders become spread out as they hustle down a hill, while the rear riders become bunched as they slowly climb a hill. The riders look like an accordion, stretching out going down the hill and bunching up as they go uphill.

Riding with Other Trail Users

You likely have to interact with other users on the trail. Friendliness and respect are the best ways to increase horseback acceptance on the trail. Although standard rules of conduct exist, in some situations common sense and courtesy prevail.

- **Be aware of your surroundings.** Watch for other trail users ahead, behind or to the side of you, so you can be prepared to direct your horse accordingly. Although hikers, bicyclists and motorcyclists, including all-terrain vehicle riders, should yield to horseback riders and move off the trail, not everyone is familiar with that cardinal rule. When another user yields to you, acknowledge the effort by smiling, waving and saying, "Thank you." Remember that those manners, or a lack thereof, make positive or negative impressions. If another user doesn't yield to you, see if you can get off the trail. Arguing with a rude hunter or four-wheeler enthusiast is pointless and only makes matters worse. If you can't get off the trail, politely ask the person to move to the side, then stop while you pass. To help prevent your horse from spooking

187

You never know what type of backcountry enthusiast you'll encounter, so prepare your horse for anything.

If you open a gate, be sure to close it in case there's livestock on the land. The rest of the group should wait for you to close the gate before riding away.

at the "monster" on the trail, ask the other user to stand where your horse can see him, and then start a conversation with the person before passing.

- **Pass politely.** When you encounter another user on the trail, heading toward you, pass on the right, single file. When approaching another user from the rear, first ride along behind for a bit to give the slower person a chance to find a place to pull off and allow you to pass. Smile, acknowledge the effort by saying, "Thanks, beautiful day," or "Good-looking horse," or by making some friendly gesture. If the slower party doesn't move off the trail after a moment, make sure you can see far enough ahead to clear the person without meeting an oncoming group. Call out "passing on your left" to warn others of your approach. If someone passes you, ride to the right side of the trail and stop. As you pass another user, or are passed, monitor your horse's body language for signs of disobedience, such as pinned ears or a raised leg, and be ready to discipline him quickly if he attempts to bite or kick. If you pull off the trail, don't line up with your horse's hindquarters toward the trail like a kicking gantlet waiting for victims. Either have

your horse's body parallel to the trail or completely off the trail. (To correct a kicking horse, see Chapter 17.)

- **Yield to uphill users.** In all cases, downhill users must yield to uphill users. This is the only time other users besides horseback riders might have the right of way.

- **Stand out.** If you ride in hunting zones, schedule rides for late morning or after noon when possible, as wildlife and hunters are most active during early morning and evening, and visibility is poor during those times. During hunting season, don reflective or bright orange clothing and tack, and make noise so hunters are aware of your presence and don't mistake you or your horse for wildlife.

- **Watch for motor vehicles.** On your ride you might be required to cross or travel near a road. Ride single file, as far from the pavement's edge as possible, making it easy for vehicles to pass. Don't assume that the driver notices you and will slow down or share the road. If you must ride on a road, take a tip from motorcyclists: Use the entire lane to prevent an uninformed person from whizzing past you. Ideally,

Abide by trail regulations and ride only where allowed.

Place all garbage in trash receptacles or haul it home with you.

you've already taught your horse the spook-control skills outlined in Chapter 8, "Ride Through the Fear," so spooking shouldn't be an issue. Still, monitor your horse for signs of spooking, such as tension and nervousness. Recognize that your horse could spook from a plastic bag into the path of a speeding vehicle. If that happens, turn his head toward the spooky object to keep him away from the oncoming vehicle.

Respect the Environment and Inhabitants

- **Obtain permission.** Before you ride on private land, obtain permission from the landowner or lessee. Trespassing is not only illegal, but it also conveys a lack of respect. Remember that your actions represent all trail riders.

- **Close gates.** If you open a gate, make sure you close it. Livestock often graze on forest and public lands, and the owners don't want their stock roaming outside that area.

- **Be respectful of other people's property.** Out of respect for ranchers and residents, hone your team-penning skills at home or in the practice pen, not on grazing live-

stock. If you pass sheds or outbuildings, stay away from them. Leave alone tools, equipment and other objects that might belong to an area farmer or rancher. And, don't trespass near homes and into yards, or near backcountry camps.

- **Tie tactfully.** In some areas, it's illegal to tie your horse to a tree. Check with the local forest service for regulations in any area you ride. For safety and to prevent tree damage, use hobbles, hitching posts when available or tie your horse using tree-savers, crossties or picket lines. If possible, use portable corrals or pens provided to contain horses.

- **Follow the signs.** Ride only on designated horseback trails, marked with a sign of a stick figure on a horse. Shortcuts destroy vegetation and encourage other users to take the alternate route, too. Furthermore, you could get lost if you get off the trail.

- **Pick up trash.** Use trash receptacles at the trail head, or pack out all trash you bring into the forest to preserve the environment for others to enjoy. The impression you make on other trail users and park-service representatives paves the way for other horseback riders.

19

TRAIL TACK

As with any discipline, trail riding has its own set of tack considerations. Although about any tack style goes for trail riding, your gear should hold up to the stress of rugged riding, plus keep you and your horse comfortable. Here's a rundown of my trail-tack preferences.

Note: I buy the bulk of my veterinary supplies from a discount veterinary-supply catalog. For emergencies or special needs, I visit a local farm-and-ranch-supply store. I've purchased tack from various sources, including online auctions and reputable Web sites.

Saddle
- **Options:** At my facility I have about 25 saddles, including those for reiners, team ropers, calf ropers, barrel racers,

A flex-panel system has been incorporated into the Mike Kinsey Trail Saddle design.

endurance riders, trainers, and even a few English saddles. Most have traditional trees, but there are a few with flex-trees and a few with flex-panels. When buying a trail saddle, I look for safety, horse and rider comfort, durability and value, respectively.

- **Safety:** You don't want a saddle to come apart as a horse flounders through a bog, crosses a log or navigates a steep incline. A poor-quality rigging, or a poorly made or neglected saddle can come apart under the stress of trail riding, thus risking danger to you or your horse. I see more and more cheaply made saddles on the market. I hear some folks talk about a few hundred dollars being a big investment. Keep in mind: A visit to the emergency room is likely to cost a couple thousand dollars. What's your life worth?

- **Horse comfort:** I expect my trail horses to deal with discomfort and continue to do

their jobs. I don't expect them to deal with sore backs from poor-fitting saddles, nails protruding from the fleece of cheaply constructed saddles, and galling due to hard or filthy cinches. Such isn't training; it's just abuse. Adding pads to build a base for a wide saddle on a young horse or one with low withers somewhat makes up for poor fit, but doing so causes other problems. To stabilize the saddle with too much padding, folks pull the cinch very tight. Some young or intolerant horses react negatively to this, biting or kicking. Instead, buy a saddle in a width that fits your horse.

A technical advance that has won me over during competitive and cross-country riding has been the flex-panel system. Don't confuse this with a flex-tree. I'm not yet a fan of the flex-tree. We have four at our facility, and I'm still riding and considering. In the flex-panel system, flexible panels, or skirts, connect with ball hinges to a solid tree to conform to different

A dropped rigging helps keep the fenders from hanging up on the saddle underneath while going up- and downhill.

horses' backs. Having veterinary judges looking, prodding and poking every 10 miles or so during a 60-mile timed ride provided me with valuable insight into the superiority of the flex-panel system although some cheaper flex-panels are unsafe.

I don't recommend trail riding when using "treeless" saddles or pads with stirrups. Full-sized adults doing so reflect a combination of ignorance and abuse. There is a reason such tack is prohibited by knowledgeable cross-country and competitive trail organizations.

- **Rider comfort:** This is a very personal issue. Folks with bad knees might want the easy-turning stirrup. Folks who don't ride much might be comfortable with extra cushion. Some folks prefer barrel saddles with higher cantles or the cutaway from a reining, cutting or training saddle. Going to a saddle shop with a variety of

styles, brands and fits is a good place to start. Recognize the difference between a salesman and an older or more experienced horseman who can help you with fitting.

- **Durability:** Durability is a factor of not just the saddle, but also the type of riding you do. If you ride a decently trained horse on wide, well-maintained trails with gradual slopes, your demand on the saddle is much less than someone, like me and my assistants and students, who traverse rugged country and work with green mounts. Our trail saddles must stand up to horses falling against trees and rocks, and flipping over in the training pen. We need saddles to which we can dally a youngster and know the saddle won't come apart. We've had horns come loose, riggings tear apart, stirrups ripped off, trees broken and leather chewed. Brand-name roping saddles tend to use heavier leather, heavier rigging and sturdier trees than off- or

When buying a used saddle, check the saddle for a broken tree. Place your knee in the saddle's seat, shifting your weight onto that leg. Pull up on the horn and cantle. If the saddle bends, it has a broken tree.

Turn the saddle on its side and press down on the edge of the cantle and pommel to ensure they're durable and intact.

no-name brands, so also tend to be heavier, making saddling difficult for a small or short person.

- **Value:** I find a used brand-name saddle offers more bang for the buck than a new, no-name saddle. For our student program and training program, I buy used, name-brand roping saddles. Used barrel saddles are generally good buys and popular with our students because of the fit. Calf-roping saddles are generally good buys for the training program, plus they're relatively inexpensive and very rugged, but not as popular with the students because of the low cantle. Team-roping saddles are a compromise for durability and a secure fit, but it's tough to get good value because of their high demand. When buying a used saddle, learn to recognize a broken tree, so you don't get home with a weak saddle.

  For retraining mature horses that might want to flop around due to resistance issues, I use team-roping saddles because they hold up well to rough use, and they hold their wholesale value well. The heavy-duty tree can withstand a horse falling in the trailer or on a ride, and can take a blow to the horn from a horse flipping over in the training

pen, and I can pony a young horse without fearing the rigging will rip apart. There are several high-quality production saddles in the $1,000 to $1,500 range on the market. Finding an older saddle often is smart, as nowadays many manufacturers focus more on profit margins than quality.

  For starting young, thin horses, I opt for a saddle with a narrow tree. The young horse's narrow back needs the narrow tree to keep his withers or backbone from being rubbed. The supposed advantage of a training saddle is the extra dees attached for fitting reins, or other training considerations. For half the price, an older roping saddle with the same tree works just as well, and we use the rear dees to tie reins or other items.

  Although Cordura® and synthetic saddles are easy to clean and handle, most just aren't durable enough to withstand the rugged conditions in which my students and I ride.

- **Recommendation:** I have been so impressed with the flex-panel system "giving" to the horse that I've incorporated it into the Mike Kinsey Trail Saddle, designed by Timberline Saddle Company.

The Mike Kinsey Trail Saddle has a combination of features that I like. The saddle has a smaller horn for less interference with the rider's hands and reins, but still functional enough for leading a packhorse. Placing nylon under the leather creates a lighter saddle that retains its strength. Because this saddle sits lower than most flex-panel saddles, it has the stability that I want. The unique fenders easily twist to keep pressure off the knees during those longer rides. The dropped rigging addresses one of my pet peeves—fenders "hanging" on the rigging when transitioning up- and downhill. These fenders swing freely. The cantle offers enough support for me when my horse flounders up those soupy trails, but is short enough that I have freedom to move my pelvis to avoid the lower back pain that I get with so many saddles. Lighter than a traditional western saddle, but still heavy enough to be rugged, this work of art is the most comfortable saddle I have ever ridden. An unexpected benefit has been that I now use the saddle in the arena when developing performance prospects.

Stirrups

To select stirrups, I consider the same points outlined in the saddle section. I opt for oversized, solid plastic stirrups, because the larger models distribute concussion across a wide area, have a flat platform to keep the foot from flexing and help prevent large feet from hanging too far off the edge. All of these things enhance rider balance. Furthermore, the heavy-duty plastic is lightweight, durable and easy to clean. Plus, no parts are susceptible to corrosion except the keeper bolt, and it's galvanized to reduce rust. Avoid sharp edges on a stirrup that can cut into a horse should he fall with the stirrup under him.

Tapaderos

When we train and ride in the mountains, especially in the wintertime, I believe in tapaderos. These stirrup covers provide increased safety by preventing a foot from sliding through the stirrup, causing a hang-up. In the wintertime, tapaderos partially protect your feet from cold air, water and snow. In the brush, tapaderos help prevent your toe and foot from becoming hung up.

The flat platform of this stirrup style offers comfort, safety and stability in the saddle.

Tapaderos protect your feet from the elements.

Helmets

On a new horse or a surly stallion, I wear a helmet. As I get older and stiffer, I don't ride as well. More and more I wear a helmet. My assistants also wear them when start-

There is a variety of helmets on the market, including lightweight and adjustable models with vents to keep your head cool.

When tightened correctly, a neoprene cinch won't pinch or gall. It's also easy to rinse off with a hose.

ing young horses or retraining horses. My students under 18 wear them on or around the horse at all times. I encourage my older students to wear helmets during lessons, and demand that my novice students wear helmets on trail rides. When my daughter first started riding problem horses for me, she wore a well-fitting hockey helmet with full-face guard. Don't let your pride cost you an injury that can be prevented.

Cinches

Neoprene front cinches are reliable, non-galling and easy to clean. The benefit of cleaning ease is to help prevent disease spread. For these reasons I won't use a rope, fiber or felt cinch. I dislike treating "girth itch" or any other fungal or bacterial infection. These infections can cause anyone to lose a couple weeks of training or riding.

I like the extra security a rear cinch provides as I ride down embankments or steep slopes. The rear cinch prevents the saddle from tipping forward, should a rider lose his balance and pitch forward against the swells. If you use a rear cinch, make sure you have a connector strap between the front and rear cinches, to keep the rear cinch from slipping back and into your horse's flank. Make sure your horse is comfortable with the feel of a rear cinch before you hit the trail. Riding with a loose rear cinch because "the horse does not like it snug" is asking for trouble. I keep my rear cinch as snug as any roper. If you can't get your horse to accept a snug rear cinch, take it off. Going downhill is not the time to have your horse start bucking when the rear cinch goes tight.

Blanket or Pad

For normal half- to three-hour rides I recommend a heavy, acrylic, oversized blanket. The acrylic is easy to wash and dry. We hose off these blankets if they aren't too dirty, and machine-wash them occasionally. The oversized blankets allow adequate drape under 17-inch saddles. For longer rides, 1-inch-thick, textured neoprene pads work well. Although they occasionally squeak when you ride, they stay in place slightly better than nontextured pads. The best pads I have used, albeit the most expensive, are the Supracor® pads. These pads are the same material found in wheelchairs and under bedridden patients. These are another

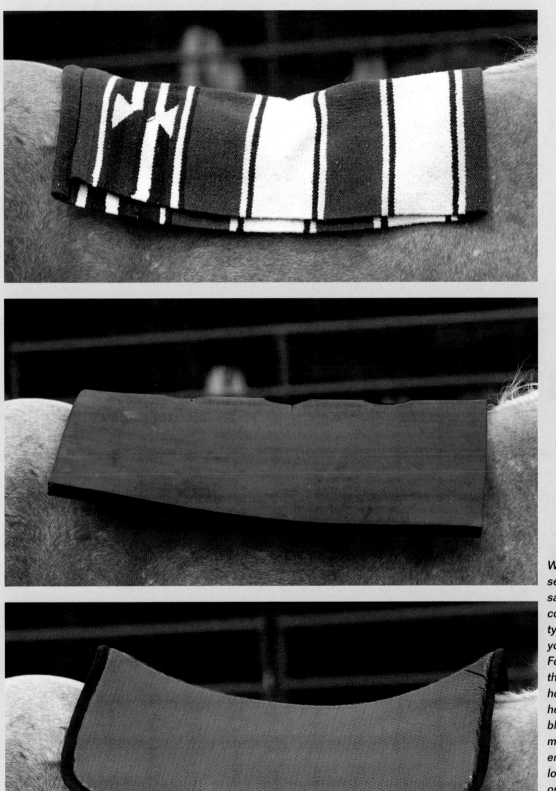

When selecting a saddle pad, consider the type of ride you're taking. For rides less than three hours long, a heavy, acrylic blanket (top) might be enough. On longer rides, opt for a 1-inch-thick neoprene pad (middle) or a Supracor pad (bottom).

piece of equipment that hard cross-country riding has demonstrated to be effective.

Breast Collar

I prefer contoured leather breast collar because they hold up well to heavy use. If you notice chafing under the breast collar, try a neoprene breast collar. Such models are self-lubricating and can prevent chafing. Avoid fleece-lined breast collars, as they're difficult to clean. As a result, they can harbor bacteria and fungus, contributing to the spread of disease and skin infections, especially when used on multiple horses. I have used vinyl-coated nylon breast collars in cross-country rides to my advantage.

The breast collar that matches the Mike Kinsey Trail Saddle is leather with an easy-to-clean, neoprene underside.

Breeching and Crupper

These are useful on a mutton-withered horse that doesn't carry a saddle well when negotiating severe down-slopes. I prefer to use a rubber-covered nylon crupper, as opposed to a breeching, because the crupper has fewer straps that can become snagged or hung along the trail. Nylon breeching generally requires less maintenance than leather and has a longer life. If I need more security, then breeching would be the choice.

Make sure you work your horse at home under control and build to using either a crupper or breeching on slopes. Horses occasionally do object to either, and might do so by kicking or bucking. Buy a crupper or breeching through tack shops and equine-supply catalogs that stock outfitting gear. Make sure the crupper has no sharp edges to wear a sore on the horse.

On my packsaddles, only the heavy-duty breeching will do. I have been impressed with the vinyl-coated nylon breeching.

Bridle

I prefer a headstall with browband and throatlatch. This style provides good security against losing the bridle in the brush. To avoid having to worry about loose screws, I replace all Chicago screws with ties, commonly called "water ties." Or, if I use the screw, I treat the screw threads with Loctite, a thread-sealing product available at hardware stores. A drop of bright red fingernail polish also works and leaves behind an indication that the screw has been treated.

Some folks prefer halter-bridle combos, and I suspect they can be useful in some situations. However, when I tie a horse, I tie prepared for a battle, and I haven't seen any combination bridles as rugged as my handtied rope halters (see below).

I ride with 6- to 7-foot, heavy harness-leather split reins, depending on the horse's size. I ride with 6-foot reins on small horses and 7-foot reins on large ones. I have tried 8-foot reins and find them too long for my comfort. Not only are these harness-leather reins durable, they also enable me to direct-rein my horse effectively. Plus, I can pop his rump with the rein ends, if necessary, to get his attention and discipline him. All of my reins have high-quality scissor snaps so I can easily remove the reins to slide on a halter to tie the horse, work him in a round pen or to adjust

A breeching or crupper is an important component of a pack horse's gear, but you can also use a crupper on a saddle horse or mule that has shallow withers that don't hold a saddle in place.

This headstall with a browband and throatlatch will stay put on the horse's head.

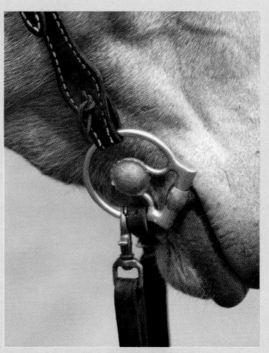

I ride most of my horses in snaffle bits, but I always fasten a curb strap to each ring to prevent pulling the bit through a horse's mouth.

I modify the design of most hobbles to fit my program. I cut off the chain secured to each dee ring, and fasten the two dees together.

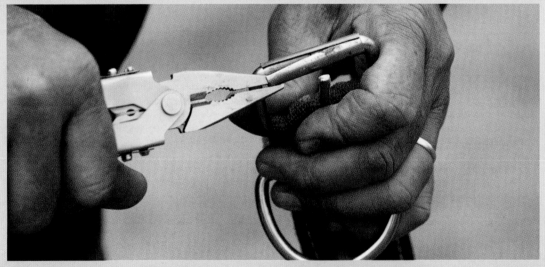

Remove the metal roller on the hobble buckle to prevent abrading your horse's legs.

rein length. When I have a group of folks on a trail ride, I generally carry an extra pair of reins, in case someone breaks theirs. I don't like braided reins for trail riding, because some of the strength comes from the core, and the core isn't visible or inspectable, so you risk sudden breakage.

Hobbles

I use 2-inch-wide nylon hobbles, always with neoprene or felt lining. This style eliminates some of the leg-rubbing I notice with unlined nylon or leather hobbles. Plus, in damp, muddy training environments, leather and cotton get wet, causing hobbles to stretch, then break. The chain and swivel mechanism is too long for most of my needs, so I cut off the chain to the dee-ring, and fasten the two dees together with a locking link. Make sure the buckle is at the end of the hobble strap, with the dee placed in an inch or so. If a dee at an end of the hobble has the buckle placed inward, pass on the hobbles. Having the dee at the end means it takes longer to get the hobble on a horse, exposing a handler to more danger when dealing with a problem horse. I also take heavy needle-nosed pliers and remove the roller from the buckle since it can cause abrasions on a fussy horse.

Halter and Lead Rope

I use handtied, $5/16$-inch braided nylon rope halters. The thin diameter causes discomfort if a horse pulls back; in turn, he

A rope halter is not only a restraint device, but also a training tool. Its thin diameter applies pressure to the horse's nose, teaching him to yield to pressure.

203

These nylon saddlebags are a good size for most rides, and they have a place to store water bottles.

learns to yield to the pressure or stand still. Thick halters are bulky and don't offer the same training benefits.

For most horses I use 10-foot, $5/8$-inch, braided-nylon leads. That way, after tying it to the halter, I have a 9-foot lead rope. The rope's diameter is thick enough to grasp, strong enough to hold the most determined horse that pulls back, yet still thin enough to tie easily. For stallions or problem horses, however, I prefer a 12-foot lead. Long leads can be awkward to handle, but they're safer than short leads; if a horse spooks on a short lead, the handler risks getting injured.

Tip: Never turn out a horse wearing a halter. If you must turn out your horse in a halter, use a style that breaks away if the halter becomes tangled.

The flexible bars on this packsaddle adjust to a horse's back and offer several options for hanging panniers.

Here is the same packsaddle with the panniers attached.

Water and Necessities' Carriers

Although pommel bags are great to pack items on seasoned mounts, I avoid them on horses in training. The bulk of the bags interferes with my hands and reins. Instead, I prefer saddlebags, which I fasten on the rear of the saddle with saddle strings. This leaves room to tie a halter or raincoat to the rear cinch or dees.

Packsaddles

Through the years I have used sawbucks and the newer flex-bar packsaddle that works similar to the flex-panel saddle. I would never go back to a sawbuck or a Decker. These flex-bars come with a variety of options to hang panniers. Need a second opinion? The Long Rider's Guild also recommends these flex-bar packsaddles.

Learn what items are essential to pack for a trail ride, and which items you might be able to leave in the trailer.

20

SADDLEBAG CHECKLIST

You've heard the old adage, "If a horse can get hurt, he will." Nowhere is there more opportunity for injury and emergency situations than on the trail. With a little planning and a well-stocked saddlebag, however, you can handle most minor circumstances. And, if an emergency occurs, you and your horse have a better chance of reaching safety. To help you hit the trail prepared, I've compiled a list of my personal saddlebag components, plus handy items to include if there's room.

Keep in mind that "first aid" is just that—basic care given at the scene until more extensive measures can be taken. I'm a minimalist: I don't overload a horse with heavy saddlebags. Instead, I take only what I need to survive until I can reach the trailer and then get the help I need.

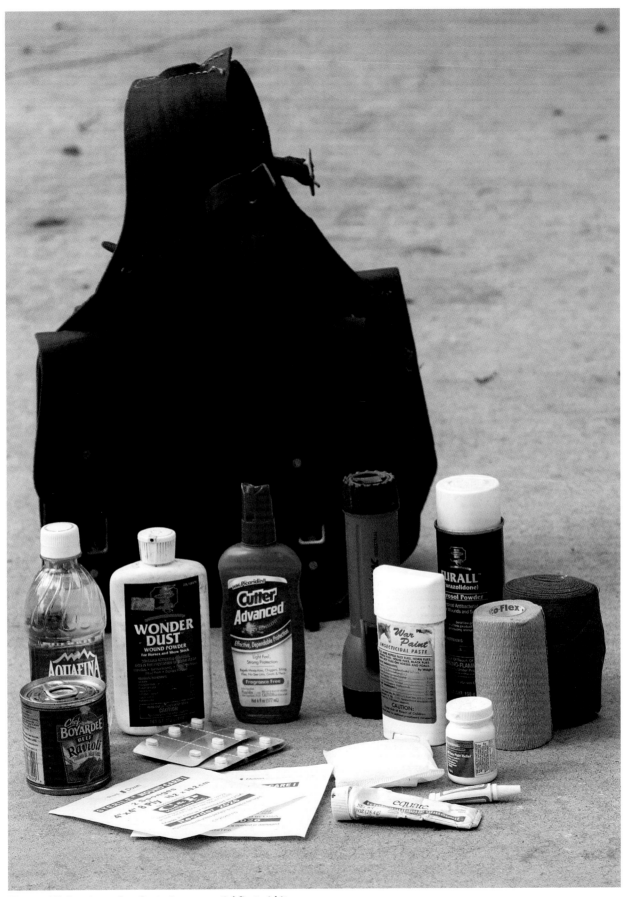

This saddlebag is perfect for toting essential first-aid items.

Packing Perspective

I stock three first-aid kits: One is marked with a red-cross symbol and contains first-aid essentials I pack on the trail. The other kit is an extensive collection of first-aid items for eye injuries, serious wounds, etc., which I leave in the trailer. In case there's room for more items, I pack a nice-to-have bag, filled with helpful yet nonessential items. Keep in mind that if you're lost or injured in a nearby forest, you probably can be found within 24 hours, although being lost or severely injured in remote, mountainous areas might mean surviving for days. In the latter case, the first item of survival gear is a knowledgeable guide with an extensive pack list and medicine chest.

Basically, deciding what to pack in your saddlebag is a matter of personal preference and necessity. Here, I focus on what I consider essential and nice-to-have items for a day ride. Remember: I take a minimalist approach; you might desire more.

Saddlebag Essentials

- **Disposable elastic bandages:** These stop bleeding long enough to return to the trailer, plus seal and protect wounds, and help keep them clean. Because bandage adheres to itself, it doesn't require pins or tape.

- **Wound powder:** Sprinkle powder on wounds to help clot minor bleeding.

- **Nonstick gauze pads:** Use to clean or cover wounds, or to apply pressure to bleeding areas.

- **Feminine-hygiene pads:** Use to stop bleeding from gunshot or for other large wounds.

- **Water:** Most backcountry trails don't have potable water for humans.

- **Iodine water-treatment tablets:** Water treatment tabs keep the humans functioning.

Nice-to-Have Items

- **A small rasp:** Use to bevel a splitting hoof.

- **Nippers:** Use to pull a mangled shoe or to trim a splitting hoof.

- **Needle-nose multipurpose tool:** This offers several handy tools in one unit to pick feet; relace and repair broken tack; cut branches, vines and wire; tighten tack screws and more. This is an item I carry every time I leave the house.

- **Benadryl liquid in a calibrated bottle and bee-sting or allergy medication:** Use to relieve insect bites, bee stings and allergy attacks.

- **Extra set of reins:** Use in case a rein breaks or as a tourniquet in a pinch.

If you have room in your saddlebags, pack farrier tools, an extra pair of reins, a hoof boot, a hoof pick and a slicker.

Even when you go on a short day ride, be prepared for any kind of horse or human emergency.

- **Flashlight:** You need this if your horse becomes injured or you become lost after dark. It might be wise to pack an extra set of batteries, too.

- **Pocketknife:** Make sure it's sharp to cut rope in case your horse becomes tangled.

- **Cell phone:** Check for coverage in the area you're riding. If there is no coverage, save that space for another item.

- **Rain gear:** Include a slicker and hat cover.

- **Insect repellent:** Pack horse and human varieties for pest protection.

- **Antacid and pain reliever:** Use to prevent pain, discomfort and inconvenience along the trail.

- **Compass and topographic map:** If you know how to use these tools, they can help prevent you from getting lost.

- **Antiseptic spray:** Use to help prevent infection in minor scrapes and wounds.

- **Disposable wipes:** Clean scrapes, burns, tears, etc., and these are useful for other personal-hygiene needs.

- **Nonperishable food:** Trail mix and jerky are compact, nutritious choices. My group, which includes younger students, doesn't leave home without Tootsie Roll Pops.

- **Temporary shoe:** Although I haven't found the ideal slip-on plastic shoe, some riders have had good luck substituting duct tape for a manufactured hoof boot.

Items in Case You Get Lost

My first suggestion: Look at maps and plan your route so you don't get lost. Consider the orientation of major rivers, ridges and roads. As you ride, note the lay of the land, the rivers and ridges. If you become disoriented, consider backtracking. Once you realize you're hopelessly lost, don't expend energy going around in circles. Remain in an area where you can be seen. Listen for a search party and be ready to signal for help. Items you might wish to carry include:

- **Matches and fire starter:** Store in a plastic bag so they stay dry. Be careful not to start a forest fire.

- **Whistle:** Blow to call for help.

- **Signal mirror:** Learn how to signal for help ahead of time.

- **Space blanket:** This very lightweight blanket provides warmth by reflecting heat back to the body. Plus, it also makes an excellent signaling device due to its reflective quality.

- **Iodine tablets:** Use these to purify stream or river water.

- **Freeze-dried rations:** Mix with water for a meal while you wait for help to arrive.

PROFILE: JENNIFER DENISON

Jennifer Denison

Jennifer graduated from Colorado State University in 1995 with bachelor's degrees in journalism and equine science. She began her equine-journalism career at *Horse & Rider*. In 2002, she joined the *Western Horseman* staff and is currently a senior editor and the Cowboy Culture editor for the magazine.

One of Jennifer's first major assignments for the magazine was producing the 12-part *Backcountry Basics* series, which culminated in this book. Finding the perfect source for the series was a challenge, until she was referred to Mike Kinsey.

"Mike was just the horseman I was looking for," Jennifer recalls. "He's one of the few professional trainers who is devoted to helping recreational riders, and his no-nonsense approach to training and horsemanship is so important for establishing a safe, reliable partnership with any horse, whether it's a trail horse, ranch horse or competitive horse."

The series won an American Horse Publications Award in the Instructional Series category, one of many AHP awards Jennifer has earned for her work. Her first book, *Bringing Up Baby*, which she co-authored with clinician John Lyons, was based on an award-winning series published in *Horse & Rider*.

Jennifer has owned horses for more than 20 years and has used them in various capacities, including showing, barrel racing, trail riding and working cattle. She and her husband, Robert, live on a small acreage outside Woodland Park, Colo., where they pasture two horses used for trail riding, roping and ranch work.

Mike and Jennifer stand along the banks of the Chatooga River in South Carolina. The motion picture Deliverance, *as well as a portion of this book, were shot in the scenic area.*

Books Published by
WESTERN HORSEMAN®

ARABIAN LEGENDS
by Marian K. Carpenter
280 pages and 319 photographs. Abu Farwa,
*Aladdinn, *Ansata Ibn Halima, *Bask, Bay-Abi,
Bay El Bey, Bint Sahara, Fadjur, Ferzon, Indraff,
Khemosabi, *Morafic, *Muscat, *Naborr, *Padron,
*Raffles, *Raseyn, *Sakr, Samtyr, *Sanacht, *Serafix,
Skorage, *Witez II, Xenophonn.

BACON & BEANS
by Stella Hughes
144 pages and 200-plus recipes for delicious
Western chow.

BARREL RACING
Completely Revised
by Sharon Camarillo
128 pages, 158 photographs and 17 illustrations.
Foundation horsemanship and barrel racing skills for
horse and rider with additional tips on feeding, hauling and winning.

CALF ROPING
by Roy Cooper
144 pages and 280 photographs. Complete how-to
coverage of roping and tying.

CHARMAYNE JAMES
ON BARREL RACING
by Charmayne James with Cheryl Magoteaux
192 pages and 200-plus color photographs. Training
techniques and philosophy from the most successful barrel racer in history. Vignettes that illustrate
Charmayne's approach to identifying and correcting barrel-racing problems, as well as examples and
experiences from her 20-plus years as a world-class
competitor.

COWBOYS & BUCKAROOS
by Tim O'Byrne
176 pages and more than 250 color photograps.
From an industry professional, trade secrets and the
working lifestyle of these North American icons. The
cowboy crew's four seasons of the cattle-industry year,
Cowboy and buckaroo lingo and the Cowboy Code
by which they live. How they start colts, handle cattle,
make long circles in rough terrain and much, much
more, including excerpts from the author's journal.

CUTTING
by Leon Harrel
144 pages and 200 photographs. Complete guide to
this popular sport involving cattle and from an award-
winning, cutting-horse industry professional.

FIRST HORSE
by Fran Devereux Smith
176 pages, 160 black-and-white photos and numerous
illustrations. Step-by-step information for the first-
time horse owner and/or novice rider.

HELPFUL HINTS
FOR HORSEMEN
128 pages and 325 photographs and illustrations. *WH*
readers' and editors' tips on every facet of life with
horses. Solutions to common problems horse owners
share. Chapter titles: Equine Health Care; Saddles;
Bits and Bridles; Gear; Knots; Trailers/Hauling
Horses; Trail Riding/Backcountry Camping; Barn
Equipment; Watering Systems; Pasture, Corral and
Arena Equipment; Fencing and Gates; Odds and
Ends.

IMPRINT TRAINING
by Robert M. Miller, D.V.M.
144 pages and 250 photographs. How to "program"
newborn foals.

LEGENDARY
RANCHES
By Holly Endersby, Guy de Galard, Kathy
McRaine and Tim O'Byrne
240 pages and 240 color photos. Explores the cow-
boys, horses, history and traditions of contemporary
North American ranches. Adams, Babbitt, Bell, Crago,
CS, Dragging Y, Four Sixes, Gang, Haythorn, O RO,
Pitchfork, Stuart and Waggoner.

LEGENDS 1
by Diane C. Simmons with Pat Close
168 pages and 214 photographs. Barbra B, Bert,
Chicaro Bill, Cowboy P-12, Depth Charge (TB), Doc
Bar, Go Man Go, Hard Twist, Hollywood Gold, Joe
Hancock, Joe Reed P-3, Joe Reed II, King P-234,
King Fritz, Leo, Peppy, Plaudit, Poco Bueno, Poco
Tivio, Queenie, Quick M Silver, Shue Fly, Star Duster,
Three Bars (TB), Top Deck (TB) and Wimpy P-1.

LEGENDS 2
by Jim Goodhue, Frank Holmes, Phil Livingston
and Diane C. Simmons
192 pages and 224 photographs. Clabber,
Driftwood, Easy Jet, Grey Badger II, Jessie James,
Jet Deck, Joe Bailey P-4 (Gonzales), Joe Bailey
(Weatherford), King's Pistol, Lena's Bar, Lightning
Bar, Lucky Blanton, Midnight, Midnight Jr, Moon
Deck, My Texas Dandy, Oklahoma Star, Oklahoma
Star Jr., Peter McCue, Rocket Bar (TB), Skipper W,
Sugar Bars and Traveler.

LEGENDS 3

by Diane Ciarloni, Jim Goodhue, Kim Guenther, Frank Holmes, Betsy Lynch and Larry Thornton, 208 pages and 196 photographs. Flying Bob, Hollywood Jac 86, Jackstraw (TB), Maddon's Bright Eyes, Mr Gun Smoke, Old Sorrel, Piggin String (TB), Poco Dell, Poco Lena, Poco Pine, Question Mark, Quo Vadis, Royal King, Showdown, Steel Dust and Two Eyed Jack.

LEGENDS 4

Various Authors

216 pages and 216 photographs. Blondy's Dude, Dash For Cash, Diamonds Sparkle, Doc O'Lena, Ed Echols, Fillinic, Harlan, Impressive, Lady Bug's Moon, Miss Bank, Miss Princess/Woven Web (TB), Rebel Cause, Tonto Bars Hank, Vandy, Zan Parr Bar, Zantanon, Zippo Pine Bar.

LEGENDS 5

by Alan Gold, Sally Harrison, Frank Holmes and Ty Wyant

248 pages, approximately 300 photographs. Bartender, Bill Cody, Chicado V, Chubby, Custus Rastus (TB), Hank H, Jackie Bee, Jaguar, Joe Cody, Joe Moore, Leo San, Little Joe, Monita, Mr Bar None, Pat Star Jr., Pretty Buck, Skipa Star, and Topsail Cody.

LEGENDS 6

by Patti Campbell, Sally Harrison, Frank Holmes, GloryAnn Kurtz, Cheryl Magoteaux, Heidi Nyland, Bev Pechan and Juli S. Thorson
236 pages, approximately 270 photographs. Billietta, Caseys Charm, Colonel Freckles, Conclusive, Coy's Bonanza, Croton Oil, Doc Quixote, Doc's Prescription, Dynamic Deluxe, Flit Bar, Freckles Playboy, Great Pine, Jewels Leo Bars, Major Bonanza, Mr San Peppy, Okie Leo, Paul A, Peppy San, Speedy Glow and The Invester.

LEGENDS 7

by Frank Holmes, Glory Ann Kurtz, Cheryl Magoteaux, Bev Pechan, Honi Roberts, Heather S. Thomas and Juli Thorson
260 pages and 300-plus photos. Big Step, Boston Mac, Commander King, Cutter Bill, Doc's Dee Bar, Doc's Oak, Gay Bar King, Hollywood Dun It, Jazabell Quixote, Mr Conclusion, Otoe, Peppy San Badger, Quincy Dan, Rey Jay, Rugged Lark, Skip A Barb, Sonny Dee Bar, Te N' Te, Teresa Tivio and War Leo.

NATURAL HORSE-MAN-SHIP

by Pat Parelli
224 pages and 275 photographs. Parelli's six keys to a natural horse-human relationship.

PROBLEM-SOLVING, VOLUME 1

by Marty Marten
248 pages and more than 250 photos and illustrations. How to develop a willing partnership between horse and human and improve hard-to-catch, barn-sour, herd-bound and spooking horses and trailer-loading, water-crossing and pull-back problems.

PROBLEM-SOLVING, VOLUME 2

by Marty Marten
231 page with photos and illustrations. A continuation of Volume 1. How-to training techniques for halter-breaking; hoof- and leg-handling, neck-reining and trail-riding problems; cinchy and head-shy horses. Sound approaches to trail riding and working cattle.

RAISE YOUR HAND IF YOU LOVE HORSES

by Pat Parelli with Kathy Swan
224 pages and 200-plus black-and-white and color photos. Autobiography of the world's foremost proponent of natural horsemanship. Pat Parelli's experiences, from the clinician's earliest remembrances to the opportunities he's enjoyed in the last decade. Bonus anecdotes from Pat's friends.

RANCH HORSEMANSHIP

by Curt Pate with Fran Devereux Smith
220 pages and more than 250 color photos and illustrations. How almost any rider at almost any level of expertise can adapt ranch-horse-training techniques to help his mount become a safer more enjoyable ride. Curt's methods to help prepare rider and horse for whatever they might encounter in the round pen, arena, pasture and beyond.

REINING, Completely Revised

by Al Dunning
216 pages and 300-plus photographs. Complete how-to training for this exciting exciting event from one of the winningest horsemen ever.

RIDE SMART

by Craig Cameron with Kathy Swan
224 pages and more than 250 black-and-white and color photos. Craig Cameron's view of horses as a species and how to develop a positive, partnering relationship with them, along with solid horsemanship skills suited for both novice and experienced riders. Ground-handling techniques, hobble-breaking methods, colt-starting, high-performance maneuvers and trailer-loading. Trouble-shooting tips and personal anecdotes about Craig's life.

RIDE THE JOURNEY

by Chris Cox with Cynthia McFarland
228 pages and 200-plus color photos. Insightful training methods from Chris Cox, 2007 and 2008 The Road to the Horse Champion. Step-by-step techniques for gaining confidence and horsemanship expertise, and for helping your equine partner reach his full potential in the arena, on the ranch or down the trail. From theory to practical application, equine psychology, natural head-set, horsemanship basics, collection and advanced maneuvers. Chapters on trail riding, starting colts and working cattle.

RODEO LEGENDS

by Gavin Ehringer
216 pages and vintage photos and life stories of rodeo greats. Joe Alexander, Jake Barnes, Joe Beaver, Leo Camarillo, Clay O'Brien Cooper, Roy Cooper, Tom Ferguson, Bruce Ford, Marvin Garrett, Don Gay, Tuff Hedeman, Charmayne James, Bill Linderman, Larry Mahan, Ty Murray, Dean Oliver, Jim Shoulders, Casey Tibbs, Harry Tompkins and Fred Whitfield.

STARTING COLTS

by Mike Kevil
168 pages and 400 photographs. Step-by-step procedure for starting colts.

THE HANK WIESCAMP STORY

by Frank Holmes
208 pages and 260-plus photographs. The biography of the legendary breeder of Quarter Horses, Appaloosas and Paints.

TEAM ROPING WITH JAKE AND CLAY

by Fran Devereux Smith
224 pages and more than 200 photographs and illustrations. Solid information for fast times from multiple world champions Jake Barnes and Clay O'Brien Cooper. Rope-handling techniques, roping dummies, and heading and heeling for practice and in competition. Sound advice about rope horses, roping steers, gear and horsemanship.

TRAIL RIDING

by Janine M. Wilder
128 pages and 150-plus color photographs. From a veteran trail rider, a comprehensive guide covering all the bases needed to enjoy this fast-growing sport. Proven methods for developing a solid trail horse, safe ways to handle various terrain, solutions for common trail problems, plus tips and resources for traveling with horses. Interesting sidebars about Janine's experiences on the trail.

WELL-SHOD

by Don Baskins
160 pages, 300 black-and-white photos and illustrations. A horse-shoeing guide for owners and farriers. Easy-to-read, step-by-step information about how to trim and shoe horses for a variety of uses. Special attention to corrective shoeing for horses with various foot and leg problems.

WIN WITH BOB AVILA

by Juli S. Thorson
Hardbound, 128 full-color pages. World champion Bob Avila's philosophies for succeeding as a competitor, breeder and trainer. The traits that separate horse-world achievers from also-rans.

WORLD CLASS REINING

by Shawn Flarida and Craig Schmersal with Kathy Swan
160 pages and 200-plus color photos. The sources' complete training program that catapulted them to reining stardom. Horse selection, training philosophies, basic foundation principles, exercises and training techniques for reining maneuvers, plus show preparation and competition strategies.

Western Horseman, established in 1936, is the world's leading horse publication.
For subscription information: 800-877-5278.

To order other *Western Horseman* books:
800-874-6774 • Western Horseman, Box 7980, Colorado Springs, CO 80933-7980.

Web site: **www.westernhorseman.com**.